THE GOD CONFUSION

ALSO AVAILABLE BY GARY COX

THE GOD CONFUSION

Why nobody knows the answer to the ultimate question

GARY COX

Bloomsbury Academic
An imprint of Bloomsbury Publishing Inc

B L O O M S B U R Y
NEW YORK • LONDON • NEW DELHI • SYDNEY

Bloomsbury Academic

An imprint of Bloomsbury Publishing Inc

1385 Broadway
New York
NY 10018
USA

50 Bedford Square
London
WC1B 3DP
UK

www.bloomsbury.com

**BLOOMSBURY and the Diana logo are trademarks of
Bloomsbury Publishing Plc**

First published 2013
First published in paperback 2015

Library of Congress Cataloging-in-Publication Data
A catalog record for this book is available from the Library of Congress.

ISBN: HB: 978-1-6235-6429-2
      PB: 978-1-6289-2970-6
      ePub: 978-1-6235-6980-8
      ePDF: 978-1-6235-6921-1

Typeset by Fakenham Prepress Solutions, Fakenham, Norfolk NR21 SNN
Printed and bound in the United States of America

Men despise religion. They hate it and are afraid it may be true.

(Blaise Pascal, *Pensées*, p. 4)

CONTENTS

INTRODUCTION

In a book I wrote a few years ago called *How to Be a Philosopher* I tackle the so-called tree question: 'When a tree falls over in a forest and there is no one around, does it make a sound?' One approach to this question considered in that book is that of the idealist philosopher, Bishop George Berkeley.

Berkeley argues that there are no material things, only collections of ideas that are perceived by a mind. So-called things, as collections of appearances, must appear to a mind in order to have any reality. Hence Berkeley's famous maxim, 'To be is to be perceived.' This immediately raises the problem of how a tree or any other object continues to be when there is no one perceiving it.

Berkeley offers what is in one sense a very neat solution to this problem. A tree that I am not currently perceiving continues to exist because *God* perceives it! God, being God, perceives everything all the time and so maintains the objective existence of the entire world simply by thinking about it. God continually thinks all those collections of ideas we call things and so prevents them from being merely subjective and from going out of existence when we are not perceiving them.

How to Be a Philosopher ends by saying that Berkeley's answer to the tree question would be unequivocal: the tree exists – as a collection of ideas – and it makes a noise as it falls because God hears it. I describe this as a 'beautiful solution' to a host of perplexing problems regarding the existence and nature of the external world. It *is* a beautiful solution, but its beauty is only skin deep, because beneath it a vast and knotty problem remains. The philosophical soundness of Berkeley's theory requires nothing less than an absolute proof of God's existence!

The inconclusive conclusion to *How to Be a Philosopher* sets the agenda for this book, the agenda being to conduct a philosophical investigation into questions concerning the idea and existence of God. Questions concerning God are never far from the true philosopher's mind, whatever side he or she takes in the various interminable God debates. To be a true philosopher is to be bothered about God one way or another, and every philosopher worth his or her salt knows the main arguments and positions in what has come to be known as the *philosophy of religion*.

When people start discussing big philosophical questions concerning the nature and origins of the universe, the meaning or meaninglessness of it all and so on, God invariably crops up somewhere in the debate. The debate then seeks to affirm him or deny him or, as most often happens, leaves a big question mark dangling over him. Certainly, for many centuries, philosophy was concerned almost exclusively with talking about God. In medieval times, Western philosophy was more or less indistinguishable from Christian theology. It had become little more than a tool for advancing theological positions to the greater glory of a God that no sane person dared to doubt the existence of. Today, many philosophers find philosophy an equally effective tool for advancing atheism.

This book does not evangelize for God and religion or, indeed, for atheism, secularism and science. It simply explores in an objective and unbiased way what philosophers have said over the centuries about the idea and nature of God, his relationship to the world and his existence or non-existence. It concludes, as its title suggests, that agnosticism is the only tenable *philosophical* position, but it does not evangelize for agnosticism or advocate an Agnostic Church, for it is perhaps not wise to live and die as an agnostic. I hope that what I mean by this last rather cryptic remark will become clear by the end of the book.

I will be keeping my personal views out of proceedings as much as possible, but personally, at the time of writing this, I am indeed an agnostic. These days, 'agnostic' is taken simply to mean a person who is undecided or in doubt as to whether God exists or not. More precisely, it refers to a person who holds that certain knowledge of a supreme being, ultimate cause, etc. is impossible. Well then, I am currently an agnostic in both the simple and the precise sense.

Certainly, I do not buy into many of the ideas that some religious fanatics have offered me on my doorstep over the years, and I do not see how it is possible for me to *choose* to commit myself to believe what they say if I find that in thinking rationally about what they say I just do not believe it. Surely, it belongs to basic common sense that belief should not be a matter of what a person *wants* to believe, but a matter of what reason and evidence dictate.

To take a small example, I was once told on my doorstep that one day the kingdom of God will be established on Earth and that the lion will lie down with the lamb. Doubting Thomas that I am, I asked what the lion would eat. The reply was that the lion would eat straw. I may not know anything for certain, but in light of all the myriad, interconnected beliefs that I hold about the everyday world on the grounds of sound empirical evidence, the claim that one day the lion will lie down with the lamb and eat straw is utter nonsense. I just do not believe it and cannot believe it and I would insult my own intelligence if I were somehow able to persuade myself to believe it.

Of course, to be fair, not all religious thinking is as silly and way-out as the example I have taken here. Far from it. Some theists are philosophically extremely sophisticated, just as some atheists are extremely obtuse. Belief in God, and fundamentalist beliefs in the literal truth of anti-scientific, religious mumbo jumbo, may be two completely different things.

As for atheism, to be an outright atheist is to assert that one *knows* for sure there is no God. But I am pretty sure that nobody knows this for sure. As I tried to show in *How to Be a Philosopher*, philosophy reveals that there is very little if anything that we can know for absolute certain – hence the sub-title of that book: *How to Be Almost Certain that Almost Nothing is Certain*. Arguably, all claims to knowledge beyond mere truisms, such as, 'A father is a male parent', are subject to doubt and uncertainty.

I have always argued that it is my *scepticism* that prevents me from being an atheist, from committing myself to such a strong position of certainty. A sceptic is a person who doubts, and just as various philosophical doubts and problems that I am aware of prevent me from asserting the strong theistic position that God definitely exists, so various other philosophical doubts and problems prevent me from asserting the strong atheistic position that God definitely does not exist. Of course, we have yet to explore what is meant by 'God' or, indeed, what is meant by 'exists' with particular reference to God. This will be our starting point in Chapter 1.

Some philosophers have argued, quite sensibly, that to find God, to acquire heart felt belief in him, a person must set aside reason and scepticism in favour of *faith*. A person must set aside all the various picky little doubts that make reasoned belief in God so difficult if not impossible, and instead undertake to approach life in such a way that in time he acquires genuine religious convictions. In other words, a person must take a leap of faith in the hope that if he starts *behaving* as though he believes, he will eventually believe. This is interesting stuff, and I certainly relate to the moral concerns and mortal anxieties of those great thinkers such as Pascal, Tolstoy, Kierkegaard and James who write of the pressing need to take a leap of faith. Yet still the sceptical philosopher in me questions the whole notion of faith.

As a Sartre scholar I am constantly reminded of Sartre's view that all faith is bad faith. That faith is allowing oneself, for motives of psychological comfort, to be convinced when one is barely persuaded. I will also never forget what my old philosophy professor, Anthony Manser, once said to me as an undergraduate, blowing smoke as he pointed at me with his pipe: 'Faith is believing what you know ain't true'. Certainly, faith is believing, or pretending to believe, or hoping to believe, or needing to believe, what it is not possible to be sure about. There is no need for faith in the face of sound evidence or proof. I will return to the issue of faith later on, particularly in the conclusion to this book.

It is an interesting question in itself to ask why people are so interested in the God question. Mention God in mixed company and straightaway people dive into a debate about whether or not God exists, arguing for their respective theism, atheism or agnosticism. Perhaps their main concern is to respond to organized religion, which tends to preach that a person is in serious trouble if he or she does not *believe*. That is, if he or she does not subscribe to what religion offers. The clear message is that to fail to believe in God is to go against God. More to the point, it is to risk missing out on eternal life, or even to condemn oneself to eternal damnation in the fires of hell.

Clearly, to threaten people with eternal damnation if they do not sign up to the *creed* has always been one of the main ways in which religious organizations recruit members and keep them obediently towing the line. Those who believe in God feel relieved that they have settled the question on the safe side. Meanwhile, the atheists are taking a risk but refuse to be threatened. As for agnostics, many of them feel they ought to make more effort to believe, just to be on the safe side, just in case a punishing God really does exist.

If I am airing my personal views here in order to largely set them aside for the rest of the book, I have to say I frown upon the hypocrisy and intolerance of organized religion that insists on selling the disease along with the cure: the disease being guilt and fear and the cure being absolution. What has always irked me most about organized religion, however, is the idea of the jealous or punishing God, the God who gets angry if humans do not believe in him and worship him: the spiteful God, the petty God. This idea makes no sense to me, although I confess to an irrational fear of it, instilled into me since childhood by society generally.

Why would a supreme being capable of creating the universe be so petty as to be *offended* that a poor, confused creature scurrying about on one of his myriad planets does not believe in him? Equally, why would a supreme being be so petty as to be *pleased* that another of those creatures believes in him and worships him? Surely, a God worthy of the name would no more care that he was worshipped than I care that my cats are grateful when I feed them. Many religious groups like to emphasize that their God is a loving God, but often they cannot help seeing this love as extremely conditional.

Seemingly, the view that many religious people have of God is rather narrow-minded, limited and crude. They see the creator of a billion galaxies as caring what they eat, what they wear and how they grow their hair. I dare say that people who think like this have been brainwashed by those who pretend to be concerned for their spiritual well-being but are really only concerned with controlling and exploiting them. This issue is explored in Chapter 2 where we examine, amongst others, the views of the philosopher Karl Marx.

As a reaction to the rule-bound pettiness of organized religion I am fond of repeating something I once read in the novel *Foucault's Pendulum* by Umberto Eco. 'Someone – Rubinstein, maybe – once said, when asked if he believed in God: "Oh, no,

I believe … in something much bigger."' (*Foucault's Pendulum*, p. 620). For the sake of brevity, I boil this down to: 'I do not believe in God, I believe in something much bigger.' As we shall see, unlike many religious people whose belief in God is a petty-minded, dispassionate, sheep-like affair, many of the great philosophers and theologians of history have also believed in 'something much bigger' when it comes to God.

Fortunately perhaps, this book is not particularly concerned with organized or even disorganized religion and has little to say about actual faith communities and their religious prejudices, practices, ceremonies and rituals. This book is simply concerned with investigating those areas of the philosophy of religion that deal with the meaning of the term 'God', the origins and importance of the idea of God and the various arguments for and against the existence of an entity corresponding to that idea. Enough material to keep an army of deep thinking philosophers and theologians lost in contemplation for centuries, and certainly enough to keep us intellectually engaged in the relatively few pages that follow.

1

The idea of God

A few hundred years ago, so historians tell us, nobody seriously doubted God's existence, just as today nobody seriously doubts the existence of gravity. The idea of God was fundamental to each person's understanding of the universe and their place in it. So, the most pressing philosophical question back then was not, as it is now, 'Does God exist?', but rather, 'What is God like?' It is a good idea to set aside the question of God's existence for the time being and ask instead, as did the philosophers of old, 'What is the nature of God?'

On the face of it, this seems a strange approach to take, for if God does not exist then surely he has no nature. Should we not at least attempt to get clear about God's existence or non-existence before we start enquiring into his nature? The problem with doing this, the problem with starting with the admittedly pressing and important question, 'Does God exist?', as most people do in their impromptu theological debates, is that what is meant by 'God' in these debates often remains unclear.

I have listened to debates on the subject of God, I have even taken part in a few, where it gradually emerged that the participants did not all mean the same thing by the term 'God'. As far back as the ancient Greeks, philosophers have insisted that before a philosophical debate is allowed to proceed, the participants should clearly define their key terms, so that when the debate is in full swing everyone is barking up the same philosophical tree and not different trees in forests several miles apart. As philosophers ignore the advice of the ancient Greeks at their peril, certainly with regard to the ground rules for conducting a philosophical discussion, we will seek to define what we mean by 'God' before moving on to consider his existence and so on.

Interestingly, regardless of whether or not God exists, it is possible to say a great deal about the nature of God, or rather, a great deal about what the term 'God' means. The guiding question at this stage is, 'What would a being worthy of the name *God* have to be like?' Or, to put it more precisely, 'What characteristics or attributes must necessarily belong to the very idea of God?'

The supreme being

The essentials of God's character profile, it turns out, can be logically and rationally unfolded with relative ease if we begin, as medieval philosophers did, with the assertion that God is the *supreme being*, or that 'God' *means* 'supreme being'.

That God is the supreme being surely stands to reason, for if there was another being in the universe or beyond it more supreme than God then that being would in fact be the supreme being – would in fact be God – and not the first being you thought of. Indeed, what is really being said here is that the term 'God' refers to the most supreme being that anyone can possibly conceive of. In his *Proslogion* (*Discourse on the Existence of God*), the Italian-born medieval philosopher and Archbishop of Canterbury, Saint Anselm, describes God as, 'Something than which nothing greater can be thought' (*Proslogion*, p. 7). So, what are the *specific* attributes of a being than which nothing greater can be thought? What are the *divine attributes*, as they have come to be known in philosophical and theological circles?

Before reading my response to the above question, you might like to pause for a while and do some of your own philosophizing by reflecting on what *you think* the divine attributes of a supreme being must be. When you reach the end of this paragraph, put this book down for a while. Go and make a cup of tea or take a walk in the garden. Probably best not to watch TV or start messing around on Facebook, as such in-your-face activities will distract you and destroy your contemplative mood. But whatever you do, you must ponder, like some pious medieval monk pacing the cloisters of a monastery, the divine nature of the one true God. Make a list of divine attributes on paper or in your head. When you come to read on, see how many of the divine attributes on your list are listed below. Perhaps you will think of one or two that I have missed. Perhaps, when you have read what I have written, you will decide that one or two of your items are not divine attributes after all....

The divine attributes – perfect in every way

I have already referred to God as 'he'. This is not because I think God is a he. If God exists, there is no reason to suppose that he is either a he or a she. Indeed, reflecting on the divine attributes strongly suggests that God would be non-gendered. To refer to God as 'he' is simply to follow a language convention. English only has two personal pronouns, and to refer to God as 'she', or even 's/he', would be equally false and contrived. I could refer to God as 'it', but this would be even more unsatisfactory than 'he' or 'she'. The idea of God, it seems, must be the idea of a being that is in some sense personal, because a God devoid of all personal attributes, such as intellect and will, would be a far lesser God than one with these attributes.

To say that God is personal or has personal attributes, however, is not to say that God is a person in the ordinary sense of the word. Persons, human persons for example, change over time and have physical bodies, whereas God does not change and does not have a physical body.

God cannot change because, quite simply, he is perfect. As God is and must be the supreme being he must already be perfect in every sense, otherwise his imperfections would render him less than supreme. He cannot change the way in which he is perfect because he is already perfect in every way. Neither can he change into something more perfect, as he must already be maximally perfect. And certainly, he cannot become less perfect and still continue to be God.

As God is unchanging he cannot have a physical body in the manner of an ordinary person. Physical bodies are made of matter and matter changes over time. Even if God had a very special physical body that did not change or decay, this body would nonetheless limit him to one place at a time and to one point of view or perspective at a time. God, as we shall see shortly, cannot be limited in this way and still be God. To conclude, God is *personal* but he is not a *person* in the way that the term is ordinarily understood and used.

A supreme being, though he is not a person in the ordinary sense, must nevertheless have the attribute of mindedness, otherwise he would be unaware of his own existence or the existence of anything else, and would lack an attribute possessed even by finite, earthly creatures such as humans and dogs. The mindedness of a supreme being worthy of the name would have to be a *perfect* mindedness. His perfect intellect would consist of perfect rationality, knowledge and wisdom, while his perfect will would consist of perfect goodness and power. A perfect intellect knows everything, it has infinite knowledge and understanding, it is *omniscient* (all knowing). A perfect will can do everything, it has infinite power, it is *omnipotent* (all powerful).

There has been a lot of heated theological debate over the centuries about what exactly God's omniscience and omnipotence consist of. When it is said that God is all knowing, does this mean that he knows absolutely everything, or that he knows everything that it is *possible* to know? For instance, if I have a genuine free will then, arguably, it is not possible for God to know what I am going to do tomorrow, given that I have not yet *chosen* to do it. If he does know what I am going to do then my doing it must be predetermined, an essentially unfree and unchosen act. Of course, not knowing what it is impossible to know is not really a limit to knowledge. It makes perfect sense to say that God's omniscience consists in knowing everything that it is *possible* to know because not knowing what is unknowable is not a form of ignorance.

Similar things can be said about God's omnipotence. Does God have the power to do absolutely anything, or simply the power to do anything that it is *logically possible* to do? Can God, for example, make 4 + 4 = 7 or create a triangular square? Some have insisted against reason that God can do such things because he is infinitely powerful, while others have argued more sensibly that it is not possible even for God to do the illogical because the illogical is only ever to do with contradictions in statements and never to do with actual situations. Importantly, the latter group go on to argue that not being able to do the illogical is not a limit to God's power.

It is possible to say 'A triangle is a four-sided shape' but it is impossible to actually think of a four-sided triangle, let alone create one. The illogical is not a realizable state of affairs. It is nothing but contradiction. To put it another way, the *limits* of logical possibility are not *limitations* in the ordinary sense of the word, because there is nothing and can be nothing beyond what is logically possible.

A contradiction does not describe a possible, if weird, state of affairs. It merely expresses what must be entirely ruled out as being logically impossible. So, it makes perfect sense to say God's omnipotence consists in his being able to do anything that it is possible to do. God can move mountains with ease because it is entirely possible, logically speaking, to move mountains. But he cannot create a four-sided triangle because there can be no such thing. As there is no such thing, and can be no such thing, being unable to create such a thing is not a limit to God's power.

An essential aspect of God's perfect will is said to be its perfect goodness. God, it is argued, always wills what is morally good. Many philosophers, including Plato and Augustine, have identified perfection with moral perfection, viewing evil as a lack, failing or imperfection. For God, to will evil, to do evil, would be to lack perfection and so not be God. God, it seems, must always and unavoidably will what is good. The notion of God's perfect goodness raises greater philosophical difficulties than the notion of God's perfect power, which we have hopefully clarified by arguing that God can do whatever is logically possible.

If God must always will what is good, then it appears God's will is constrained by morality; it appears morality constitutes a power over him. And if morality constitutes a power over him how can he be all powerful? It can be argued that because God *is* perfect goodness then it is logically impossible for him to do what is morally wrong. This limitation, however, appears to be different from his 'inability' to do the illogical and create, for example, a three-sided square. It appears to be a *genuine* limitation. After all, mere mortal, human persons can do what is morally wrong. Are we to say that a mere human person can do what God cannot do; that God is more constrained in what he can do, at least in this respect, than you or I?

In attempting to get out of at least some of these difficulties, some philosophers have argued that God can do what is morally wrong if he wants to, but that he always chooses not to. The aim of this argument is to make God's unrelenting goodness a product of his free will rather than an unavoidable product of his eternally fixed nature. But still the problem remains of how a perfectly good being could have the *option* of choosing to do wrong, even if he never actually took that option, and still remain a perfectly good being. God cannot take the option that is theoretically open to him and remain God.

Whatever God actually does the issue remains of what he *ought* to do. Even if he always does good as a matter of choice, God is nonetheless doing what he *ought* to do, acting in accordance with a set of moral principles that constitute a law over him. If morality is superior to God then God is not omnipotent. If, on the other hand, God is superior to morality, then morality and goodness must be whatever God decides they are. By this line of reasoning God remains good whatever he wills, whatever he does, because he alone decides what is good. The problem now, however, is that 'good' loses all meaning, all association with objective, independent moral *principles*, and 'God is good' is reduced to a mere truism that can say nothing meaningful about the nature of God.

The dilemma that arises from considering which is higher, God or morality, was first identified by the ancient Greeks. It has come to be known as the *Euthyphro dilemma* because it is explored in detail in Plato's dialogue *Euthyphro*. In the dialogue, Socrates cleverly ties poor Euthyphro in knots in order to expose the dilemma. 'We shall soon be better able to judge, my good sir. Consider this question: is what is pious loved by the gods because it is pious, or is it pious because it is loved?' (Plato: *Euthyphro*, 9a–10b, p. 31). We will return to the Euthyphro dilemma when we consider the *moral argument* for God's existence in Chapter 3.

While we are on the subject of God's perfect goodness, it is worth raising a question that people have asked for millennia and continue to ask everyday: If God is perfectly powerful and perfectly good, if he always wills good, then why is there so much evil and suffering in the world? The problem raised by this question is known as the *problem of evil*. It is one of the great problems of theology. Its importance is such that the whole of Chapter 4 is dedicated to it.

The divine attributes – everywhere all the time

'Omni' means 'all' and God is certainly omni this and omni that. Apart from being all knowing and all powerful, God is said to be *omnipresent*. God is said to be everywhere because if there

(unnecessary). Interestingly, many modern versions of the Bible have instead the words 'I am who I am', a formulation that surely fails to convey God's all important philosophical point regarding his own self-sufficiency.

We need to halt proceedings here for a moment and take a good look at the path we have suddenly gone down. The agenda for this chapter is to explore what belongs to the very *idea* of God, setting aside questions of God's existence or non-existence until later. But we seem to have shifted from talking about the *idea* of God to the *existence* of God. Many philosophers have thought this shift is unavoidable, arguing that because the very idea of God is the idea of a necessary being, then God must necessarily exist. Anselm and others argue that God simply cannot be thought of as not existing. On the face of it, this seems quite a convincing argument, as we have quite easily developed the idea that God cannot not exist by merely reflecting on his other necessary attributes. The argument that existence must be an attribute of the supreme being is known as the *ontological argument*.

The ontological argument is one of the best known arguments for God's existence and has been put forward in various forms by many philosophers over the centuries. Unlike other arguments for God's existence, it depends entirely on pure reason and logic. It is a so-called *a priori* argument, *a priori* meaning prior to or apart from experience. Clever argument though it is in many ways, it is fair to say that the ontological argument does not work. The reasoning it involves has been shown by various philosophers to be erroneous. What precisely is wrong with the ontological argument is explored in detail in Chapter 3 in the section dedicated to it. Meanwhile, we must press on with our exploration of what belongs to the *idea* of God.

God, as I said, is omnipresent. He is in all times and places in the universe. He is everywhere and everywhen. He is not, however, identical with the universe. The idea that God just is the whole universe is known as *pantheism* (God-is-all-ism). Pantheism is a popular view these days with new-age pagans who want to get away from the Judeo-Christian idea of a distinctly existing, personal, moral God. Rather than saying something like 'I see God in this daisy', they say, 'God is this daisy, and everything else besides'.

The problem with pantheism as a so-called religious point of view is that God vanishes as a distinct, personal entity existing in his own right. What remains is an impersonal, contingent, physical universe subject to change and decay that does not have the attributes that God is said to have. In a sense, pantheism rules out God as much as atheism does. Pantheism simply tries, after ruling God out, to shoehorn him back in again by insisting that the terms 'universe' and 'God' are synonymous.

If, to be God, God must be distinct from the universe and not identical with it, God must *transcend* the universe. He must in some sense transcend both space and time. He must in some sense be above and beyond the universe and totally independent of it. The universe is not God but God's creation. The argument that the universe is God's creation follows from the view that God is necessary and self-sufficient whereas the universe is not.

The universe, the argument goes, is contingent, it need not be. Or to put it another way, everything in the universe need not be and once was not. A universe of things that need not be and once were not could not have caused itself. Neither could it have been caused by nothing. Something cannot come from nothing, or, as the pre-Socratic philosopher, Parmenides famously puts it, 'Nothing comes from nothing.' In Latin: *ex nihilo nihil fit*. This maxim has been quoted and rephrased down through the centuries by many thinkers, including Aristotle, Lucretius and Shakespeare. So, the universe must have been created by a being that must be and has always been. A necessary being that must be the *first cause* of everything that need not be and cannot cause itself. God's creativity is known as his *omnificence*. God is all creative or the creator of all.

In the previous few paragraphs my main aim was to show that God is distinct from the universe he is said to have created and not synonymous with it. You will not be surprised to learn, however, that the argument employed above has often been used by philosophers to attempt to prove God's existence. It constitutes what is called a *cosmological proof*: an attempt to deduce

God's existence from the existence of the universe as such. The cosmological arguments for God's existence are considered in detail in Chapter 3.

Arguing that God is transcendent, that he is above and beyond the universe, that he is outside of space and time, establishes him as a very remote being, as a being entirely detached from the spatio-temporal world in which humans operate. The theological standpoint of *deism* accepts that God is entirely transcendent and detached in this way. Deists insist, for instance, that God absolutely cannot intervene in his creation. He must remain entirely separate from it for it to be a true, independently existing creation and not merely part and parcel of himself.

Unhappy with the idea that God is so remote, many religious thinkers insist that God must also be *immanent* as well as transcendent. Immanence or inherence is the condition or quality of existing, operating or remaining within. As immanent, God is within the universe, within space and time, everlasting rather than eternal.

God must be transcendent in order to inhabit an eternal present in which he is not excluded from the past or the future, and in order to be distinct from the universe he created. God must be immanent so as not to be utterly remote, so as to have a relationship with people, to answer prayers and to be present in human history as a force for moral good. Interestingly, to insist that God is *only* immanent is to insist on pantheism as outlined above.

How God achieves the necessary trick of being both immanent and transcendent is often put down to his omnipotence. He just has the power to do it and that is that. We have seen, however, that God's omnipotence does not include being able to do what is logically impossible, and it would seem that being both wholly transcendent and wholly immanent is logically impossible. Not only because it involves being both wholly within and wholly beyond the universe at once, but because it involves being in two entirely distinct states at once, like being entirely black and entirely white at the same time.

Summary of the divine attributes

'God' means 'supreme being'. Regardless of whether or not a supreme being actually exists, it is possible to deduce what must belong to the very idea of a supreme being, even if his attributes, once listed, do not appear to entirely stack up.

God cannot be a person with a physical body who changes over time, but he is *personal*, with the attributes of *perfect will* and *perfect intellect*. A being with personal qualities is greater than a being without them, so being the greatest being of all, God must possess personal qualities. Both his intellect and his will are perfect, rendering him *omniscient* and *omnipotent*. Being *all knowing* and *all powerful* appears to involve knowing and being able to do whatever it is logically possible to know and do. Being unable to do the illogical does not limit God because the illogical is nothing at all.

God is also *perfectly good*, which means God must either act according to the highest, independent moral principles or arbitrarily decide what good is. If God is obliged to be good then his omnipotence is restrained by morality. If good is whatever God says it is then 'good' has no real meaning, and 'God is good' is simply an empty truism that says nothing useful about God.

God is *omnipresent*, he is in all times and places at once. God's omnipresence mean that he is not subject to time as we are: trapped in the present moment and excluded from past and future. In occupying past, present and future simultaneously, the three dimensions of time do not really apply to God. God is *eternally present*. Being omnipresent, God can have *no beginning* and *no end*. Not least, there is nothing more powerful than God to bring him into existence or to end his existence.

The idea of God is the idea of a *necessary being* that cannot be thought of as not existing. Although this point appears to prove God's existence ontologically, it does not in fact do so, as will be explained in due course. Although omnipresent, God is *distinct* from the universe rather than synonymous with it (pantheism). As God is *self-sufficient* and the universe, arguably, is not, God must be the *first cause* and *creator* of the universe.

God is *omnificent*, the creator of all that is not God. In order to be distinct from the universe and for the universe to be an independently existing creation that is not merely part and parcel of God, God must be *transcendent*. On the other hand, for God to do the good work within space and time that most religions insist he is capable of, he must also be *immanent*. Transcendence and immanence appear to be incompatible notions.

Starting with the notion of a supreme being and reflecting on what characteristics must necessarily belong to the very idea of such a being, we have managed to fathom out a reasonably comprehensive list of divine attributes. Admittedly, some or even all of these attributes are not entirely coherent, either individually or mutually, or our limited human reason cannot show that they are. But at least we now have a far clearer idea of what 'God' means and can mean than we did at the beginning of this chapter.

A general consensus over the meaning of our key term will stand us in good stead as we move forward to ponder such questions as 'Does God exist?' Recall what I said at the beginning of this chapter about the importance of making sure everyone is barking up the same tree. I would hate you to be barking and God bothering up a different tree to me.

2

The origins of the idea of God

Every society ever known has had some idea of God or gods, and every attempt to engineer an entirely secular society devoid of the idea of God has failed. So, where does this most persistent of ideas come from? Different philosophers, with radically different agendas, have offered radically different answers to this question. Before you read about *their* answers, however, I recommend you pause for a while and think about the question yourself. Make a list of as many possible answers as you can think of. Write down whatever you come up with, however odd it may seem. This is a brainstorming exercise, not a test. As always, I want you to think for yourself about an issue before you compare your thoughts with the thoughts of other philosophers. I want you to *be* a philosopher, not just read philosophy....

Descartes – the idea of God is God-given

In his most important work, *Meditations on First Philosophy*, the French rationalist philosopher, René Descartes, argues that the idea of God that each person possesses must come from God himself. God himself has given us the idea we have of him, stamped it into our minds in much the same way as a silver-smith stamps his hallmark or trademark into a silver teapot he has made. God created us, according to Descartes, and the idea we have of God is God's trademark. Not surprisingly, this argument has come to be known as the *trademark argument*.

For Descartes, the idea of God that each person possesses is *innate*. It is an inborn, built-in idea, as opposed to an idea derived from imagination or from sensory, empirical experience of the world. On what grounds does Descartes claim that the idea of God is innate rather than imagined or empirical? Well, Descartes recognizes that the human mind can think up all sorts of weird and wonderful stuff, that even the dullest person has a remarkable imagination. Being finite and imperfect, however, the human mind cannot self-generate the idea it has of an infinite and perfect being. This idea must derive from something that is itself infinite and perfect, namely God. 'I would not,' Descartes says, 'have the idea of an infinite substance, since I am a finite being, unless the idea had been put into me by some substance which was truly infinite' (*Meditations on First Philosophy*, in *Discourse on Method and the Meditations*, p. 124). Descartes is working with a certain ancient and medieval notion of causation which states that the lesser cannot by itself give rise to the greater as it simply does not have the potential, the potency, the power, to do so.

Interestingly, Descartes would argue that in the previous chapter we attained our idea of God with God's help, attained it by focusing on the *God-given* idea of God that each of us possesses. Descartes would insist that if we came up with anything in the last chapter *without* God's help, it was simply the idea of a being that is *not finite* and *not imperfect*. This is the best we can do under our own steam. But to say God is *not* this and *not* that is not to have an idea of God. A true idea of God must be positive, not negative. It must be a wholly positive conception of infinity and perfection, a wholly positive conception of God that only God himself can deliver. By the same token, our idea of God cannot be derived from empirical experience because, vast and beautiful though the universe is, it does not give us sense impressions of infinity and perfection.

It seems Descartes is right to say that the human mind cannot generate ideas of infinity and perfection. Infinity and perfection, it seems, are inconceivable. A person can think of a distance of billions of light years, but that is not to think of an infinite distance. A person can think of a ridiculously high number, higher even than the number of dollars in the US national debt, but he can always add one more to whatever number he thinks of. Similarly, I can think of a very beautiful face or a very fine meal, but I cannot think of a perfect face or a perfect meal. We have no experience of infinity and perfection, and our so-called ideas of them, our use of the terms 'infinite' and 'perfect', simply *refer* to what is not finite and not imperfect without ever amounting to actual thoughts of them.

If infinity and perfection are, as I have argued above, absolutely inconceivable in all but a negative way, then Descartes must be wrong to say we have an innate, positive idea of God's infinity and perfection. Where is that innate, positive idea? If I have such an important idea built in to my mind, why am I unable to call it up at will? Descartes might argue that only long years of devout meditation on God's nature will finally call up a positive idea of him. It is difficult to argue with this position in so far as it says that only truly holy people can get in touch with their innate idea of God and hence *know* that there is such an idea. The rest of us poor sinners must remain in the dark, taking the word of holy people on trust.

But did we not already identify the key problem with having a positive idea of infinity and perfection when we said that infinity and perfection are inconceivable? It is not that some or all of us happen to be incapable of thinking what it is possible to think, but rather that infinity and perfection are simply not thinkable, just as an infinitely high number is simply not thinkable.

Descartes needs to lay claim to the existence of an innate idea of God in the human mind in order for his version of the ontological argument for God's existence to work. Quite simply, in his view, if an innate idea of God exists in the human mind then God must exist because God must have put it there. The ontological argument is never far below the surface of philosophical discourse about God, and once again it rears its pretty head, and once again I shall defer dealing with it until later on.

Experiencing God – perception or hallucination?

It was argued above that our idea of God cannot be derived from empirical experience because the universe does not give us sense impressions of the key divine attributes of infinity and perfection. It certainly seems fair to say that we do not perceive God in the way that we see colours, hear music, smell a rose, taste an apple or feel silk. Surely, as a supernatural, metaphysical being that does not have a physical body, God cannot be perceived at all because he is just not the kind of entity that can engage with any of the five senses that are the basis of all our perceptions.

So, when people claim to have experienced a divine revelation, to have heard a voice or seen a vision or both, they must be referring to some kind of hallucination that they had rather than to something that they literally perceived with their sense organs. God, if he exists, certainly has the power to make a person think they are hearing and seeing something, the power to produce hallucinations, but this is not the same as actually hearing and seeing something, actually perceiving it via ears and eyes.

In being akin to hallucinations, so-called divine revelations are highly subjective. If your friend claims she can see an angel over there by that tree you will look over there to see if you can see it too. If you cannot see it, your friend will probably tell you that it is there, but only she can see it. If you do not doubt her sincerity, you will wonder, if you are at all questioning and rational, about the true nature of her vision. She cannot literally be seeing an angel with her eyes because if she is seeing an angel in the ordinary sense of *seeing* then you should be able to see it too if your eyes work and you are looking in the right place. So, she must be hallucinating, in which case neither of you can be sure of the source of the vision. Is it a God-given vision or a self-generated delusion? There is no way to tell, no final court of appeal.

The subjective nature of what people want to claim are direct experiences of God means that there is always an alternative, non-supernatural explanation that at least undermines the certainty that what they experienced was a revelation of the divine. It is always possible that a person was tricked, deluded or indulging in wish fulfilment at a deep psychological level. Or perhaps they simply mistook an unfamiliar but nonetheless scientifically explicable and impersonal phenomenon for a supernatural sign deliberately directed at them by God.

Take the supposed divine revelation, the vision and voice of Christ, that precipitated Paul's conversion to Christianity on the road to Damascus. The German philosopher, Friedrich Nietzsche, argues that Paul merely suffered an hallucination as a symptom of his epilepsy. The content of Paul's epileptic hallucination was simply a projection of concerns that were subconsciously playing on his mind at the time as a persecutor of Christians. 'And at last the liberating idea came to him, together with a vision, as was bound to happen in the case of this epileptic' (Nietzsche, *Daybreak: Thoughts on the Prejudices of Morality*, Book 1, Sec. 68, pp. 40–1).

The very different claim that *natural* phenomena themselves signify the divine, that the order and coherence of the universe clearly indicates God as its supernatural designer, is something we will consider in detail when we explore the so-called *teleological argument* or *argument from design* in the next chapter.

Inventing God to fill the gaps

If the idea of God is not God-given or derived from experience, then it must be an invention of the human mind. The human mind can easily build up quite a detailed idea of God simply by considering what characteristics would have to belong to a truly supreme being. The idea of God, then, can arise simply as the result of a mind game, and it was precisely this mind game that we played in Chapter 1. What is really interesting, however, is not that people can readily generate the idea of God, but rather the deep *need* they have both to generate the idea and to believe that something real corresponds to it.

The French philosopher, François Marie Arouet de Voltaire, recognized this deep need when he famously said, 'If God did not exist, it would be necessary to invent him' ('Epistle to the Author of the Book of the Three Impostors', 10 November 1770). Interestingly, this remark was not intended as the atheist slogan it has become. Voltaire believed in God and was actually *attacking* a group of atheist philosophers. Quoting himself in November 1770 in a letter to Frederick the Great (1712–86), Voltaire wrote, '"If God did not exist, he would have to be invented." But all nature cries aloud that he does exist: that there is a supreme intelligence, an immense power, an admirable order, and everything teaches us our own dependence on it' (*Voltaire in His Letters*, p. 231).

Many philosophers have argued that the idea of God arose largely as a way of attempting to explain the natural world. Not least, the idea of God has been employed for millennia in countless creation myths to explain the existence of the world as such. To say that God created the world provides a convenient answer to questions about where the world came from, and it is an answer that still seems to satisfy many people. For many people, it is still an explanation at least as good as the complex and so far incomplete *big bang theory* offered by physics. One day, physicists argue, science will fully explain how the universe began – though most people will not understand the mathematics involved – and in so doing make the notion of a creator redundant. Certainly, science has already made the notion of God largely redundant when it comes to explaining natural phenomena such as light, reproduction, weather, earthquakes and so on.

In primitive, pre-scientific societies natural phenomena were mysterious. People of course knew from experience that children resemble their parents, but they did not know why. They of course knew from experience that earthquakes involve a violent shaking and cracking of the earth and that they happen more in some places than in others, but they did not know in geological terms what earthquakes are or what really causes them. They of course knew from experience roughly what weather the seasons will bring and that a red evening sky usually means good weather the following day, but they had no idea what causes weather patterns and no real ability to predict the weather with any degree of certainty. In their ignorance, they were inclined to conclude that family resemblance, earthquakes and the change and character of the seasons are all governed by the will of God, and that a red sky at night is simply a God-given sign of good weather to come.

Meteorology, as we all know, is still not a perfect science, especially over the medium to long term, but short-term weather forecasting is now astonishingly accurate because we have a detailed scientific understanding of the atmospheric conditions that bring about fine, wet or stormy weather. When we know so clearly what causes a storm, there is no longer any need, and it no longer makes any sense to claim, as people did in the past, that God causes storms. Storms come about simply because of pre-existing physical conditions, not because God is angry or seeking to punish us. Where science does not give us control over the natural world it teaches us that some phenomena are beyond anyone's control and that, therefore, no one, human or divine, is to be blamed or praised for their occurrence.

Mankind is able to have some limited influence over the weather, seeding clouds with dry ice or silver iodide to make it rain for example, and we are increasingly blaming extreme weather on global warming caused by human industrial activity, but generally, the weather is seen as entirely independent of our actions. In explaining the weather scientifically as an entirely natural phenomenon, rather than as a series of acts of God, we are no longer moved, as people were in the past, to influence the weather by influencing God. If a personal force is made to be responsible for natural events, then it makes sense to believe it is possible to sway that personal force towards a positive intervention using prayers, offerings and sacrifices. On the other hand, if no such personal force is envisaged, only indifferent nature, then it makes no sense either to cajole or curse it.

So, believing that God controlled nature was a symptom of people's very limited empirical understanding. The idea of God can be seen as a pre-scientific hypothesis for 'explaining' the inexplicable. An idea that arose out of people's inability to scientifically explain or control all those phenomena that had such a huge and terrifying influence over their lives, from weather and infestations to sickness and disease. To use the idea of God to seek to explain what cannot be explained scientifically is to conjure up what has come to be know as *God of the gaps*.

God of the gaps is used to conveniently plug all the gaps in human knowledge. Everything, for which a practical, cause and effect scientific explanation is lacking, is attributed to the will of God, to a sign of his pleasure, displeasure or sheer capriciousness. Historically, organized religion has tended to encourage the idea of God of the gaps by discouraging scientific discovery. By reinforcing the idea that there is a God who controls nature, and by claiming to know how best to influence his will to the good, religion has long placed itself in a powerful and lucrative position when it comes to mediating between God and ignorant folk hoping to shape natural events to their advantage.

As science has explained more and more of the world, filled in more and more of the gaps in our knowledge and allowed us to intervene in nature to a considerable extent, the need to resort to God as an explanation has significantly diminished. Nonetheless, many people still believe in a God of the gaps, partly because there is still a lot that science has not explained – such as how life first began – and partly because they refuse to understand or accept some of the extremely sound explanations that science provides, such as the theory of evolution.

Many other people say that science is the reason for their lack of belief in God. Science, they argue, has not yet explained everything, but it clearly has the potential to do so. At the very least, it is absurd to suppose that there are any natural phenomena that *cannot* be explained scientifically, even if science never actually finds the explanation. Science, they conclude, makes the idea of God obsolete, certainly as a means of explaining how and why things in the natural world happen as they do. There are no supernatural phenomena, only natural phenomena science has not yet explained. There are no genuine mysteries and therefore no mysterious gaps where God might be found lurking.

Freud – God as big daddy

Sigmund Freud, an Austrian physician and psychiatrist and the founder of psychoanalysis, was a lifelong atheist. Convinced that the idea of God is a human invention, albeit a very important one, he was fascinated with the *psychological* motives people have for conceiving of God and believing so adamantly in his existence.

Freud notes that people are largely powerless in face of the overwhelming forces of nature. Given enough time and the right circumstances people can build the Great Wall of China and make deserts bloom, but the fact remains that they cannot significantly control the weather, stop volcanic eruptions, prevent earthquakes or endlessly avoid death. Despite their ingenuity and achievements, people remain very small, weak, vulnerable and mortal. Molten magma boils a few miles beneath their feet and the empty, inhospitable vacuum of outer space lies a few miles above their heads. Accidents are always waiting to happen and death always lies somewhere up ahead. Quite simply, for many people, the idea of God eases the fear we all feel in face of a hostile universe and our own cruel fate, the fear we have all felt to some extent ever since we were small, helpless children crying alone in the darkness.

The thought that there is a supremely powerful being who created us in his own image, who cares about our well-being and is actively looking after our personal interests, is, not surprisingly, hugely comforting and reassuring to many people. In *The Future of an Illusion*, Freud says, 'I have tried to show that religious ideas have arisen from the same need as have all the other achievements of civilisation: from the necessity of defending oneself against the crushingly superior forces of nature' (*The Future of an Illusion*, p. 201).

So, for Freud, mankind's obsession with the idea of God is rooted in his deep desire for a supremely powerful supernatural protector. To desire this protector is to wish for the universe to be far less harsh and indifferent than it certainly appears to be. In Freud's view, belief in God is nothing other than *wish fulfilment*, an attempt to satisfy by means of fantasy and illusion a deep desire that cannot be satisfied in reality.

Each individual person, Freud goes on to argue, does not have to invent the comforting and reassuring idea of a supernatural protector for him or herself. Civilization has already developed and refined the idea through countless generations. It is already there in the form of the detailed idea of God the Father. Men tend to be physically stronger than women and therefore most often take on the role of family protector. It is for this reason, Freud argues, that God is generally perceived as a strong *father* figure. 'My dad is bigger than your dad', boasts the frightened child confronted by his enemies, but the idea of God the Father is the idea of a dad that is infinitely bigger than anyone's dad, a dad that will adopt you and protect you in this life and the next so long as you show him sufficient humility, respect and gratitude.

Freud tends to view belief in God as rather childish, as rooted in an infantile desire for a powerful, protective father figure who will make everything all right. The main problem with this view is that many devoutly religious people are far from childish and cowardly in their approach to life. Far from retreating from the real world and trusting in God to solve every problem, they are deeply engaged in the world in a very practical, hands-on sense, helping the poor and needy and fighting the forces of oppression.

Jesus himself got his hands dirty in the service of mankind, setting an example for figures such as Martin Luther King, Mother Theresa and Desmond Tutu to follow. Similar brave, world-engaged, philanthropic figures are to be found in other religions, the Hindu civil rights and peace campaigner, Mahatma Gandhi, for example. Certainly, religious people are comforted by their belief in God, but for many it is more of a sword that strengthens their practical resolve than, as Freud suggests, a comfort blanket to hide behind.

Durkheim – God as the symbol of society

Freud sees the idea of God as arising primarily out of human need. One of the founding fathers of sociology, Émile Durkheim, also takes this view. In his book, *The Elementary Forms of Religious Life*, Durkheim identifies the idea of God, and the many religions that centre upon that idea, as making a vital contribution to social cohesion. Religion is a social glue that, like economics, politics and law, has evolved to help hold communities together. On one level, religion provides rituals and ceremonies relating to birth, marriage, harvest and death that reinforce family and community solidarity and each person's sense of group identity. On another level, the widespread fear and reverence religion inspires and demands ensures that the moral code it upholds for the regulation of social relations and interactions is largely adhered to.

Durkheim argues that the collective identity and values of a social group are conceived by the group as existing in spiritual form independently of the group. This spirit is worshipped in the form of a God or gods. Worship of a God or gods, therefore, is really worship of society itself: its laws and values, its power to protect, judge, shame and punish. Simply put, God symbolizes society.

In Durkheim's view, a society without belief in the idea of a God or gods, a society without organized worship of a higher supernatural power, a society without religion, would disintegrate. Indeed, it would not develop in the first place. Which is to say, a society without religion is not possible or even conceivable. Durkheim has an essentially positive view of the role that religion plays in our society. It is a vital engine of socialization and hence one of the cornerstones of human civilization. As he says:

> That is why we can be sure that acts of worship, whatever they might be, are not futile or meaningless gestures. By seeming to strengthen ties between the worshipper and his God, they really strengthen the ties that bind the individual to his society, since god is merely the symbolic expression of society. (*The Elementary Forms of Religious Life*, p. 171)

Durkheim's affirmative view of religion stands in stark contrast to the highly negative view of it held by the nineteenth-century German philosopher, sociologist and political economist, Karl Marx.

Marx – God as a sedative

Marx is particularly interested in what brings about and sustains the huge inequalities that exist between different social classes. Marxist theory is vast and complex – Marx's complete works take up several feet of library shelf – but very basically he argues that religion is both a symptom of social inequality and a means of obscuring it. Religion, and the idea of God that is at the core of religion, is a pressure valve that helps to alleviate the tensions caused by social injustice. Marx considers the various iniquitous socio-economic structures that have existed historically, feudalism for example, but he has most to say about capitalism.

In a capitalist society there is a relatively small group of capitalists who own the *means of production* – land, raw materials, factories, machines, investment banks and so on – and a huge number of workers who own little or nothing more than their labour. The worker is obliged to sell his labour to the capitalist on terms that are always unfair to the worker. The capitalist will not pay the worker the true value of his labour because capitalism requires that a significant amount of value be creamed off in order to endlessly grow capitalism in the form of an ever-increasing range of goods, services and investment opportunities, and in order to maintain the capitalist class in excessive wealth and luxury. Marx refers to the value that is creamed off the workers' efforts as *surplus labour value*. For Marx, the great wealth that the capitalist considers rightfully his own and is so proud of, is nothing but surplus labour value accumulated through the mass exploitation of the working class.

Marx describes the worker as *alienated* by capitalism. Not only is he separated from the full fruits of his labour by capitalism,

capitalism prevents him from becoming a fully realized, creative human being who directs his own actions. The worker's actions are dictated by the capitalist system which extracts from him the maximum surplus labour value by forcing him to be part of a mechanical production process that requires no creativity or imagination on his part. Marx notes that the all-important profit motive of capitalism is not best served by craftsmanship, whereby a person sees a reflection of his true self, his essential creativity, in what he has created.

What best serves capitalism, in most situations, is *division of labour*, the breaking down of a complex task into a series of mundane, circumscribed tasks, each task to be carried out repetitively by a person or persons. Division of labour, the assembly line, is highly efficient at maximizing output and therefore profit, but it is extremely alienating for the millions of human beings it reduces to little more than cogs in a machine.

You may be wondering by now what all this basic Marxist theory has to do with religion and the idea of God. Well, Marx argues that such an alienating, exploitative and unjust system can only be maintained if the people caught up in it are encouraged to have a view of themselves, society, authority, life and even death that is conducive to the preservation of the status quo. Concepts, stories, myths and prejudices are promoted that instil accepting, approving, respectful, unquestioning attitudes towards the existing system.

Marx and others refer to the influential concepts, stories, myths and prejudices that shape people's beliefs, attitudes and opinions as *ideology*. Ideology provides a ready-made explanation of the world and people's place in the so-called grand scheme of things. Religion, Marx argues, is central to the ideology that helps sustain our unfair society. The ideology of religion helps justify and legitimize the existing socio-economic system, the existing power structure, not least by obscuring the inequalities and methods of exploitation inherent within it.

For Marx, religion grew out of the inequality-based tensions existing between different social groups as a means of alleviating and obscuring those tensions without addressing the underlying problem of inequality itself. Essentially, religion protects the ruling class, whose privileged position depends on inequality, by sedating and intoxicating the exploited. Hence Marx's famous remark that religion is 'the opium of the people' (*Critique of Hegel's 'Philosophy of Right'*, p. 131).

Religion persuades people that worldly inequality is not important because all people are equal in the eyes of God. It tells them that they should not concern themselves with seeking equality on Earth as they will get what is owing to them when they die in the form of an eternal paradise. Indeed, their poverty itself is identified as a virtue and therefore as a passport to heaven. Religion also tells people that society is the creation of God and that each person should be satisfied with their

God-given place in its hierarchy. In the words of the nineteenth-century hymn, 'All Things Bright and Beautiful', by Mrs Cecil Frances Alexander:

> The rich man in his castle,
> The poor man at his gate,
> God made them high and lowly,
> And ordered their estate.
>> ('All Things Bright and Beautiful', verse 3, *Hymns Ancient and Modern*, second edition, 1875. More recent editions omit the verse.)

To believe that social rank is preordained by God relieves the wealthy, powerful person of any shame and embarrassment he might feel at the thought of his position, whilst relieving the poor and powerless man of any dangerous resentment.

Religion encourages people to obsess about the moral health of their own soul, to feel guilty about their personal sin as defined by religion and their failure to follow often petty religious rules. Religion thus distracts people from seeking justice on Earth and curbs their appetite for rebelling against their oppressors. Indeed, it prevents them from recognizing who their real oppressors are. Although poverty, as said, is identified as a virtue, religion, never afraid of the odd contradiction, also teaches people to attribute their distress to the Devil or their own sinful nature rather than to systematic oppression by a ruling elite.

For Marx, religion, with the idea of God at its centre, provides cold comfort, an illusion of justice in an unjust world and an illusion of security in a cruel one. It offers soothing words and something to look forward to at the end of a miserable, uncreative, unfulfilled, alienated life of drudgery and exploitation. 'Religion is the sigh of the oppressed creature, the heart of a heartless world and the soul of soulless conditions' (*Critique of Hegel's 'Philosophy of Right'*, p. 131).

Marx argues that when revolutionary changes in the economic system finally bring about an end to social inequality and alienation, religion and the idea of God, as ideological devices for making that inequality bearable, will no longer be required. Marx said, 'Man makes religion; religion does not make man' (*Critique of Hegel's 'Philosophy of Right'*, p. 131), arguing that when mankind finds his proper place in the universe, within a just and harmonious social order that he himself has established, there will no longer be any need or desire to *make religion*; to set up the idea of God as a source of illusory happiness and consolation.

So much for theories regarding the origin of the idea of God and the purposes served by that idea. It is high time we turned to the contemplation of arguments for and against the actual *existence* of a supreme being.

3

The existence of God

Does God exist? Is there a supreme being that broadly corresponds to the description given in the first chapter? I hate to disappoint readers looking to this book for some sort of final proof or disproof of God's existence, but for reasons I will make clear, the only entirely safe answer that a good philosophical sceptic can give to these questions is 'I do not know.' To assert that God either does or does not exist is almost definitely to go way beyond what philosophy, let alone science, can ever prove or disprove.

Hardly anyone doubted God's existence a few hundred years ago. Pre-scientific explanations of the world were so bound up with the notion of God that to doubt the existence of God was like doubting the existence of weather. But this does not mean that people in the past *knew* that God existed; they simply did not question, or did not know how to question, what they had been taught.

A young child who has been indoctrinated into the Santa myth by his well-meaning parents does not doubt that Santa exists, but this does not mean that he *knows* Santa exists. It is not possible for anyone to know that Santa exists because he does not exist. One cannot know what is false, only that it is false. What the child once took as convincing evidence for Santa's existence – images in books and the trusted word of his parents – becomes less and less convincing as his experience of the world grows. Eventually, his belief in Santa becomes entirely incompatible with his belief system as a whole and as such is rejected as fantastical.

God, of course, is not Santa and belief in God is not as childish as belief in Santa. Nonetheless, these days, there are plenty of thinkers who argue that belief in God is entirely incompatible with a belief system based on tried and trusted science. God, they insist, is simply an outmoded idea like witches or the four humours. As was said in the previous chapter, a God of the gaps is no longer required since science has already plugged many of the once yawning gaps in human knowledge and seems to have the potential to plug them all. However, that science can or will explain the workings of the universe, even the existence of the universe as a whole, without resorting to God, does not prove categorically that God does not exist.

Even in our scientific age there are still millions of people who claim to know for certain that God exists. In the strict sense of the word 'know', however, it is highly doubtful that they do in fact know. Often, if they are not simply parroting doctrine taught to them by their elders when they were impressionable children, these people base their claim to knowledge on a feeling of *inner certainty* that they suppose they possess, on the strength of their belief itself rather than on the strength of the *evidence* for their belief.

The problem with so-called inner certainty is that because belief itself is not evidence for what is believed in, belief by itself without any external evidence can only be wishful thinking that refuses to recognize itself as such. So-called inner certainty is not genuine certainty, it is only false certainty fabricated from a refusal to recognize, a refusal to believe, that hope is only hope and not certainty. Inner certainty has nothing to do with knowledge and everything to do with wilful ignorance. It is a form of what existentialist philosophers call *bad faith*. The kind of bad faith that, as Sartre argues, 'stands forth in the firm resolution *not to demand too much*, to count itself satisfied when it is barely persuaded, to force itself in decisions to adhere to uncertain truths' (*Being and Nothingness*, p. 91).

That I believe something, however passionately, does not make it true. What makes it true is the supporting evidence. I can close my eyes, screw up my face, clench my fists and really try to convince myself that it is raining in the street outside my window. But however much I try to convince myself, however much I try to experience conviction emotions, it will either be raining outside or not, regardless of my so-called convictions. Rain produces the conviction that it is raining, the conviction that it is raining does not produce rain. Which is to say, there is no real or meaningful conviction that it is raining other than that produced by perceiving rain.

Belief in God has always been popular and will always be popular for the psychological and sociological reasons explored in the previous chapter, but these days there is also undoubtedly a growing fashion for atheism. A number of high-profile evangelical atheists, reacting against the menacing absurdities of religious fundamentalism and extremism, are belligerently spreading the *New Atheist* gospel that God definitely does not exist and that any suggestion that he might exist is utterly ridiculous.

The problem with atheism, philosophically speaking, is that it is a very strong belief position, no less strong than theism. It claims to know beyond all possible doubt that God does not exist. But as philosophers who understand that there are strict limits to knowledge have long argued, it is not even possible to know beyond all doubt that the external world does or does not exist. Now, if I cannot even prove or disprove the existence of the desk I seem to clearly see and feel before me, then how on earth can I hope to utterly prove or disprove the existence of a supreme, transcendental being?

The healthy scepticism that is the hallmark of every true philosopher is incompatible with a commitment to atheism, just as it is incompatible with a commitment to theism. Arguably, when it comes to God, a good philosopher can only be an agnostic, the most neutral, impartial and noncommittal of creatures, his rear end welded firmly to the fence of doubt as a matter of epistemological principle. A good philosopher will certainly avoid endorsing atheism simply because he despises organized religion. The existence of God and the excesses of religion and the religious are very different issues.

The great philosophical sceptic, empiricist and master of common sense, David Hume, argues that all our knowledge is ultimately based on our sense impressions, that there is no knowledge of anything that is not ultimately derived from empirical experience. As he says, 'In short, all the materials of thinking are derived either from our outward or inward sentiment ... Or to express myself in philosophical language, all our ideas or more feeble perceptions are copies of our impressions' (*Enquiries Concerning Human Understanding*, p. 19). As God is by definition a metaphysical being inaccessible to empirical experience, we can have no impressions of him and hence no knowledge of him.

The idea of God that people have, according to Hume, in no way amounts to knowledge of him. It is simply an idea that arises when the human mind enhances, without limitation, its down to earth, empirically derived ideas of goodness and wisdom. Certainly, for Hume, because everything we know, our entire reality, is ultimately based on our sensory impressions, it is *impossible* for us to know for sure beyond all doubt whether or not a supreme metaphysical being exists.

Philosophers continue to discuss the existence or non-existence of God for the pleasure and interest of doing so, but the most astute of them are aware that it is *philosophy itself* that reveals that the existence of God simply cannot be proved or disproved by any method of reasoning known – logical or scientific. In so far as philosophy attempts to answer unanswerable questions, its primary aim in doing so is to reveal why unanswerable questions are indeed unanswerable. One of the major tasks of philosophy is to reveal the unsurpassable *limits* of human knowledge, to indicate where all scientific and philosophical reasoning ends and mysticism begins. As one of the most influential philosophers of the twentieth century, Ludwig Wittgenstein, famously concludes: 'What we cannot speak about we must pass over in silence' (*Tractatus Logico-Philosophicus*, prop. 7).

The theistic arguments

The theistic arguments lie at the very heart of the philosophy of religion and form the greater part of its agenda. Much of the history of theology is the history of the theistic arguments, just as much of the history of philosophy is the history of theology. The theistic arguments are a series of ingenious and fascinating attempts to prove the existence of God using observation, reason and logic. The various objections to the theistic arguments are perhaps even more ingenious and fascinating in that they manage to expose as false and confused what those undoubtedly wise and conscientious men who formulated the theistic arguments took to be demonstrably true and undeniable.

The failure of the theistic arguments to prove the existence of God does not, however, amount to a proof that God does not exist. The failure of the theistic arguments merely shows that God's existence cannot be proven by means of these arguments. After the theistic arguments have been set up and knocked down the answer to the question of God's existence remains as elusive as ever. Perhaps the main purpose of exploring the theistic arguments, then, is to further clarify why, in the end, the question of God's existence cannot be answered. Why, in the end, 'I do not know' is probably the only safe and honest answer, the only truly philosophical answer.

Before you explore the theistic arguments, you may like to pause as you did earlier, put this book down, take a stroll, and see if you can work out for yourself, just by thinking about it, what the theistic arguments might be. I have already hinted at some of them in the previous two chapters, which may help. It is also highly likely that you have been offered various arguments for God's existence by God botherers you have met during your life – at school, on the high street and on your own doorstep. You may even like to take this game a step further and think about what might be *wrong* with your arguments for God's existence. Set them up and knock them down, a game of philosophy skittles....

Most theistic arguments can be classified as either *ontological*, *cosmological* or *teleological* in character. Under each of these three headings there are different versions, variations, formulations and adaptations of essentially the same argument, a reflection of the development of each argument over many centuries by respective philosophers and theologians. Very basically, the ontological argument asserts that the idea of God implies the existence of God, the cosmological argument asserts that God is the uncaused cause of everything, while the teleological argument asserts that the universe shows evidence of supremely intelligent design. There is also another important argument or set of arguments for God's existence known as the *moral argument*, which asserts that the existence of morality implies the existence of God. This is often associated with an argument called the *argument from degree* which asserts that degrees of perfection imply absolute perfection, including absolute moral perfection. We will explore each of these arguments and the objections to them in turn, starting with the ontological argument.

The ontological argument

As was said earlier, the ontological argument is never far below the surface of philosophical discourse about God and keeps rearing its pretty head. This is because any reasonably intelligent person only has to ponder the idea of God and the divine attributes for a short time before he glimpses what so many thinkers have glimpsed down through the centuries: that it might be possible to extract from the very idea of God a quick, neat, logical proof of his existence. I have already taken the liberty of saying that the ontological argument – clever, captivating argument though it is – does not work, that it is erroneous, a piece of awry reasoning, a false path. I have yet to obey a golden rule of philosophy and *justify* this bold claim, but I will do soon.

To fully understand the ontological argument and what is wrong with it we need to plot its long history and consider how different philosophers from medieval times onward have formulated it, used it, criticized and rejected it.

Anselm's ontological argument

The story really begins with Saint Anselm back in the eleventh century and his description of God as, 'Something than which nothing greater can be thought' (*Proslogion*, p. 7). Note that this description is subtly different from 'The greatest conceivable being'. The greatest being that anyone can *actually* think of might not be the greatest being of all. The greatest being of all, Anselm recognizes, must be that being of which it is *logically impossible* to think of anything greater.

As we saw in Chapter 1, Anselm argues that a being than which nothing greater can be thought must have certain attributes. If, for example, you think of a being that is *very* powerful then that being is not a being than which nothing greater can be thought because it is, of course, possible for you to think of a far greater being, i.e. one that is *all* powerful. So, a being than which nothing greater can be thought must be omnipotent. By the same token, if you think of a being that exists but need not exist, a so-called *contingent* being, then that being is not a being than which nothing greater can be thought because it is of course possible for you to think of a far greater being, i.e. one that not only happens to exist but must exist, a so-called *necessary* being. So, according to Anselm, to think of God – a being than which nothing greater can be thought – is to think of a being that must exist. Or to put it another way, God cannot be thought of as not existing, and therefore must exist.

Still working with his 'nothing greater' principle, Anselm argues that a God that exists in reality is greater than a God that is a mere idea in the mind, because a God that exists in reality possesses a key positive attribute that a God that is a mere idea in the mind lacks, namely, existence. As he says:

> Surely that than which a greater cannot be thought cannot exist only in the understanding. For if it exists only in the understanding, it can be thought to exist in reality as well, which is greater. So if that than which a greater cannot be thought exists only in the understanding, then that than which a greater *cannot* be thought is that than which a greater *can* be thought. But that is clearly impossible. Therefore, there is no doubt that something than which a greater cannot be thought exists both in the understanding and in reality. (*Proslogion*, p. 7)

The same point can be made in terms of perfection. God is a being than which nothing more perfect can be conceived. A God that exists only as an idea in the mind is less perfect than a God that exists in reality because a God that exists in reality has the added perfection of existing in the most perfect way possible, existing necessarily and eternally without beginning or end.

Summarizing Anselm's position, the eminent philosopher of religion, John H. Hick, says:

> If the most perfect conceivable being existed only in the mind, we should then have the contradiction that it is possible to

conceive of a yet more perfect being, namely, the same being existing in reality as well as in the mind. Therefore, the most perfect conceivable being must exist in reality as well as in the mind. (*Philosophy of Religion*, p. 16)

Anselm had great confidence in his considerable philosophical abilities, a confidence that endured right up to his death in 1109. 'On his death-bed,' says Richard W. Southern, 'Anselm expressed a wish to live until he had finished writing on the origin of the soul, because (as he said) he did not know who would solve the problem after his death' (*Saint Anselm: A Portrait in a Landscape*, p. 372). Anselm is respected among philosophers for relying on the force of his philosophical arguments rather than the authority of Scripture, although as a medieval Christian holy man he nonetheless made constant reference to the Bible in formulating his views.

While introducing the ontological argument in his *Proslogion* he refers to the biblical 'fool' who 'says in his heart, "There is no God"' (Psalm 14.1 and 53.1). 'Fool' here means one who is morally deficient or corrupt rather than one who is an idiot. How can even a fool think there is no God, when, according to the ontological argument, to have an idea of God is to understand that God must exist? Anselm argues that the fool is confused. Although he uses the term 'God' he does not understand that 'God' means 'something than which nothing greater can be thought'. He therefore merely denies the existence of his *misconception* of God and not God himself. If he were in touch with the correct idea of God that resides somewhere in his mind then he would know that the being corresponding to that idea must exist. Anyone can utter the words, 'There is no God', but it is not possible for anyone to actually think this. If a person thinks he can think this then that is only because he is working with a false notion of God.

Anselm and Gaunilo debate

The first serious criticism of Anselm's ontological argument was made by Gaunilo or Gaunilon, a Benedictine monk of the Marmoutier Abbey near Tours, France. Gaunilo wrote a reply to Anselm entitled, *Reply on Behalf of the Fool.* Little is known of Gaunilo beyond this treatise, a great shame as the treatise reveals an extremely sharp intellect with a leaning towards empiricism, the view that human knowledge is limited to what the mind derives from sensory experience.

In his *Reply on Behalf of the Fool* Gaunilo undertakes to reduce the ontological argument to absurdity by showing that it leads to ridiculous outcomes when applied in other areas. He considers the legend of the lost island, an island supposedly somewhere in the ocean that people say 'is more plentifully endowed than even the Isles of the Blessed with an indescribable abundance of all sorts of riches and delights' (*Gaunilo's Reply on Behalf of the Fool, Proslogion,* p. 31). In short, a perfect island.

We can easily imagine the perfect island is out there in the ocean somewhere and would understand the words of a man who insisted that it can be found, even if we did not believe his words. But suppose the man insisted that he can prove by means of logic alone that the perfect island exists on the grounds that it is perfect. Employing the ontological argument he would argue that a perfect island that exists in reality is more perfect than a perfect island that exists only as an idea in the mind, because a perfect island that exists in reality possesses the additional positive attribute of existence that the perfect island that exists only as an idea in the mind lacks. Therefore, the most perfect of islands, being indeed an island enjoying all perfections, must exist.

The absurdity of this line of reasoning is that it supposes that it is possible to prove the existence of anything you can think of so long as you insist that it is perfect. Or, indeed, that it is impossible to think of anything that is perfect as not existing. But it is, of course, possible to think of the perfect island as not existing, as being a mere fantasy, and there is no contradiction involved in denying its existence. Either the perfect island exists or it does not. Its existence or non-existence can only be established by empirical means and not by means of logic. Considering the absurdity of an ontological proof of the existence of the perfect island, Gaunilo says of any person who offered him such a proof:

> If, I say, he should try to convince me by this argument that I should no longer doubt whether the island truly exists, either I would think he was joking, or I would not know whom I ought to think more foolish: myself, if I grant him his conclusion, or him, if he thinks he can establish the existence of that island with any degree of certainty. (*Gaunilo's Reply on Behalf of the Fool, Proslogion*, p. 32)

Currently, we are merely taking pot shots at the ontological argument by considering the absurdities it leads to when applied to ideas other than God. A full-blown attack on the ontological argument for God's existence will come later when we have considered the argument in its various forms. Right now, our task is to consider Anselm's reply to Gaunilo, an essay which once had the grand-sounding title, *Anselm's Apologetic in reply to Gaunilo's Reply On Behalf of the Fool*, but these days, thankfully, is simply titled, *Anselm's Reply to Gaunilo*.

The great Saint Anselm (although he was not, of course, made a saint until after his death) begins by acknowledging the intelligence of the obscure monk, Gaunilo:

> Since the one who takes me to task is not that fool against whom I was speaking in my book, but a Christian who is no

fool, arguing on behalf of the fool, it will be enough for me to reply to the Christian. (*Anselm's Reply to Gaunilo, Proslogion,* p. 36)

Anselm agrees with Gaunilo that it is absurd to attempt to use the ontological argument to prove the existence of a perfect island or any other worldly entity. The ontological argument, Anselm insists, applies only to the idea of God and works only as a proof of God's existence. This is because God alone is by definition a *necessary being*, an eternal and independent being that is not dependent on any other being for his existence. A being whose very essence is *to be*. 'I am that I am' (Exodus 3.14). Everything else is only a dependent, contingent being that need not exist and can be thought of, without contradiction, as not existing. Only God, as the only *necessary* being, cannot be thought of as not existing. Hence, to conceive of him correctly is to be certain that he exists.

If you feel that for all its apparent theological grandeur, the reasoning above is all rather circular and that the argument is presupposing and insisting upon the existence of the very thing it is purporting to prove the existence of, then you would be right. You may even feel inclined to accuse Anselm of some sleight of hand, a cunning trick with logic that you cannot quite put your finger on perhaps. This, however, would be unfair, as Anselm is sincere in his views and certainly not out to trick anyone – the man is a saint after all! He is not guilty of deception, merely confusion, and his is certainly not the only great mind to have been taken in by the ontological argument.

You doubtless have a great mind yourself, or at least a good nose for sensing when an argument is suspect, but can you yourself yet put your finger *precisely* on what is wrong with the ontological argument? It took some very fine minds indeed to finally expose the error, minds that had the advantage of being in a position to ponder deeply the arguments of the likes of Anselm and in time learn from their mistakes. Once again, I defer exposing exactly what is wrong with the ontological argument until we have considered it in its various forms.

Aquinas dismisses the ontological argument

The next major figure in the history of the ontological argument is Saint Thomas Aquinas, born in 1225, 116 years after Anselm's death. Like Anselm, Aquinas was born in Italy to a noble family. He studied the ancient Greek philosophy of Aristotle in Naples where he fell under the influence of the recently founded Dominican Order and eventually decided to join them. The Dominicans dedicated themselves to teaching and preaching to ordinary people in their own vernacular languages, particularly in the growing cities. The Dominicans sought to address a mounting concern in the Catholic Church that the word of God was not reaching ordinary people. Dominicans were expected to live simply by what they could earn from their preaching, rather than, as other orders did, from the proceeds of land and farming.

Aquinas' decision to join this new, down-market, streetwise order, rather than follow his uncle into the older, wealthier, more prestigious Benedictine Order, put him on a collision course with his family. He was placed under house arrest for two years by his own parents to prevent him from joining. One story even has it that his brothers hired a prostitute in an attempt to destroy his celibacy but he drove her away with a burning stick. All this only strengthened Aquinas' resolve to join the Dominicans and his family eventually relented.

It was a good move all round as during his lifetime Aquinas established himself as a leading Catholic theologian whose advice was often sought by the papacy. After his death in 1274 his reputation soared to even greater heights. Not only was he canonized in 1323, but his work, promoted by his followers the Thomists, became the philosophical core of Catholicism and remains so today. He is known as the Angelic Doctor and one of the more bizarre myths about him is that he could levitate, but that is another story.

The work of Aquinas brought about a shift of emphasis in Christian theology from the teachings of Augustine to the teachings of Aristotle. Having lived before the time of Christ, Aristotle was viewed as a pagan by medieval Christians and his views were only accepted when and where they harmonized with Christian orthodoxy. Readings of Aristotle were, therefore, somewhat selective. Medieval theologians rejected, for example, Aristotle's view that the world is eternal, as this clashed with the biblical account of creation. What medieval philosophers came to admire most about Aristotle was the power of his reason and logic. They saw that by and large they could use Aristotle's rigorous *methods* of reasoning and logic to refine and reinforce their Christian world-view.

Aquinas' best-known application of Aristotelian arguments and principles to Christian theology is his *five ways*, his five proofs of God's existence as contained in his most important work, *Summa Theologiae*. We will examine Aquinas' five ways in detail in due course when we come to consider the cosmo-logical, teleological and degree arguments for God's existence. Importantly, none of Aquinas' five arguments are ontological, which strongly suggests that Aquinas rejects the ontological argument.

Aquinas is convinced that God exists, on the grounds of his faith, on the word of the Bible and on the basis of non-ontological theistic arguments. He simply thinks that there can be no *ontological* proof of God's existence, at least for human beings. Interestingly, he thinks that the ontological argument works for God himself, that in his infinite wisdom God himself understands that the very idea of himself implies the existence of himself, that the statement or proposition 'God exists' is necessarily and self-evidently true. Mere finite, mortal human beings, however, with their limited understanding, particularly of God, cannot know that the proposition 'God exists' is self-evidently true in the way that they can know, for example, that the proposition 'A father is a male parent' is self-evidently true. Human beings cannot have innate, *a priori* knowledge that the idea 'exists' is part and parcel of the idea 'God'. Hence, human beings can deny the truth of the proposition 'God exists' and like the fool claim that God does not exist, without contradicting themselves.

Descartes revives the ontological argument

The fact that the great Aquinas and his followers, the Thomists, rejected the ontological argument meant that it somewhat fell out of favour among medieval philosophers. This, however, did not prevent the father of modern philosophy, René Descartes, from reviving the argument in the first half of the seventeenth century in his *Meditations on First Philosophy*.

We came across Descartes' version of the ontological argument in the previous chapter while exploring the origins of the idea of

God. Recall that according to Descartes, we each have an idea of God in our minds that must have been placed there by God because we ourselves our incapable of generating such an idea. This has come to be known as the *trademark argument* as it claims that each person's idea of God is the trademark, hallmark or stamp of their divine creator.

According to some philosophers, the trademark argument is a version of the ontological argument because it is saying that the idea of God implies the existence of God. Many other philosophers, however, argue that the trademark argument is not strictly ontological because claiming that God must exist because he is the *cause* of my idea of him is not quite the same as claiming God must exist because it is impossible to think of a supreme being as lacking the attribute of existence. The trademark argument, though it is usually explored under the heading of the ontological argument for the sake of convenience, is really more cosmological than ontological because at its heart is the notion of a lesser x – my idea of God – *caused* by a greater x – God himself. As we will see in due course, cosmological arguments hinge around certain notions of causation.

Setting Descartes' trademark argument aside, it is important to note that he also endorses the ontological argument in its pure Anselmian form. Like Saint Anselm, Descartes insists that a supremely perfect being must exist, otherwise he would lack something and so not be supremely perfect. According to Descartes, existence is an essential attribute of God, just as having three sides is an essential attribute of a triangle. John H. Hick says, 'Descartes's ontological argument claims that existence must be among the defining predicates of God' (*Philosophy of Religion*, p. 18).

The term 'predicate' refers to a quality, characteristic, attribute or property that in a statement or proposition is said to belong to a subject. For example, in the proposition 'The sky is blue', the predicate 'blue' is said to belong to the subject 'sky'. The sky is said to have the attribute of blueness. This talk of propositions, subjects and predicates is important, as it gives us a way of looking at the ontological argument that finally allows us to see exactly what is wrong with it.

Those of you who have read *How to Be a Philosopher* will recall that the ontological argument was explored in some detail in that work. This seems to be the way it is with the ontological argument. It keeps cropping up, or rather, diverse philosophical excursions inevitably run across it. It is a major philosophical landscape feature that is encountered on many a philosophical journey. In *How to Be a Philosopher* the ontological argument appeared in our path when we were considering Descartes' attempt to prove the existence of the external world. In fact, the ontological argument is the cornerstone of Descartes' attempt to prove the existence of the external world.

Descartes argues that we cannot *know* the external world is out there by means of our senses. The senses are unreliable and easily deceived. Moreover, what we believe we are perceiving may all be a dream. Rejecting the sensory, empirical route, Descartes offers a purely rationalist proof of the external world based on the existence of God. Believing he has proved God's existence by means of the ontological argument, he makes God the guarantor of the external world. God, being perfect, would not deceive Descartes into thinking there was an external world if there was not an external world. The external world, therefore, must exist as it appears to exist.

Importantly, Descartes' proof of the external world fails, and his philosophy collapses into solipsism (the view that one's own mind is all that exists), precisely because the ontological argument fails. In *How to Be a Philosopher* it was necessary to show exactly what is wrong with the ontological argument, as the cornerstone of Descartes' proof of the external world, in order to bring that proof crashing down.

Why the ontological argument fails

We need now to revisit the objections to the ontological argument made in *How to Be a Philosopher*. I mention this in order to justify the repetition, not to apologize for it. In my many years of teaching philosophy I have found that repeat, repeat, repeat is not a bad maxim to abide by, and if you have been so wise and conscientious as to have already read *How to Be a Philosopher* then you can treat what follows as useful revision.

In *How to Be a Philosopher* I showed what is wrong with the ontological argument using the necessarily true proposition 'The perfect singer has a perfect voice.' Rather than use that proposition here, however, I want us to travel, at least in our minds, back to Gaunilo's perfect island. It sounds a very pleasant place to be, if you enjoy that sort of thing. I was going to take the proposition 'The perfect island has a perfect beach', but it was pointed out to me by a friend, noted for her common sense, that an island does not have to have a beach: a skirting of sand or shingle subject to the ebb and flow of the tide. It could be cliff all the way round, and doubtless there are such inaccessible islands.

So, let us take the proposition 'The perfect island has a perfect coast.' This is necessarily true in the sense that it is a contra-diction to say 'The perfect island does not have a perfect coast.' How could the perfect island be perfect if it had a coast that was not perfect? It surely belongs to the very *idea* of the perfect island that it has a perfect coast.

None of this implies, however, that there is a perfect island actually existing somewhere in the universe. Although it is necessarily true to say 'The perfect island has a perfect coast' and a contradiction to say 'The perfect island does not have a perfect coast', there is no contradiction if we reject the *entire* proposition. That the perfect island must necessarily be judged to have a perfect coast does not mean that the perfect island exists.

Now, as we have seen, 'God' means 'a being with all positive attributes'. By definition, 'God' means 'a being that is all powerful, all knowing, everywhere, infinite and so on'. Therefore, it is a contradiction to say 'God is a being without all positive attributes'. How could an idea of God be an idea of God if it was the idea of something that was lacking in some way? It belongs to the very *idea* of God that he has all positive attributes including the attribute of existence. 'Exists' is an essential feature of the *idea* 'God'.

None of this implies, however, that God actually exists. 'Exists' is so much a part of the idea 'God' that the proposition 'God does not exist' is a contradiction. But there is no contradiction if we reject the *entire* proposition, just as no contradiction remained when we rejected the *entire* contradictory proposition about the perfect island not having a perfect coast.

Basically, the ontological argument makes an illegitimate move from saying, quite rightly, that some ideas logically imply other ideas – like the idea of the perfect island implying the idea of a perfect coast – to saying, quite wrongly, that at least one idea logically implies that a certain thing exists. That it is possible to reason from one idea to another does not mean that it is possible to reason from the idea of a thing to the existence of that thing.

As the great German philosopher, Immanuel Kant, puts it in his *Critique of Pure Reason*, in a section dedicated to showing the impossibility of an ontological proof of the existence of God, 'But the unconditioned necessity of a judgement is not the same as the absolute necessity of things' (*Critique of Pure Reason*, p. 501).

In dismissing the ontological argument and any argument that attempts to reason from the idea of a thing to its existence, David Hume, who greatly influenced Kant, argues that it is impossible to add to the idea of any thing by conceiving of it as existing. As he says:

> 'Tis also evident, that the idea of existence is nothing different from the idea of any object, and that when after the simple conception of any thing we wou'd conceive it as existent, we in reality make no addition to or alteration on our first idea. …When I think of God, when I think of him as existent, and when I believe him to be existent, my idea of him neither encreases nor diminishes. (*A Treatise of Human Nature*, p. 94)

Hume's criticism is clearly directed at the likes of Anselm, at all rationalist philosophers who maintain that to think of God as existent, as opposed to non-existent, is indeed to *increase* the idea of him to the maximum; is to think of a being than which nothing greater can possibly be thought.

Closely following Hume and Kant, the English philosopher, Bertrand Russell, argues that existence cannot be included among the attributes, properties or qualities of a thing because saying that a thing exists does not add anything to the description of that thing. An imaginary flock of seagulls has the same characteristics as a real flock of seagulls. Existence is not itself an attribute or property, or as Russell would say, *existence is not a predicate.*

In the proposition 'Cows have hooves', for example, 'hooves' is the predicate. The predicate 'hooves' adds to a description of cows. To say 'Cows exist', however, does not add anything to a description of cows. Rather, as John H. Hick argues:

> 'Cows exist' means 'There are x's such that "x is a cow" is true.' This translation makes it clear that to say that cows exist is not to attribute a certain quality (namely existence) to cows, but is to assert that there are objects in the world to which the description summarized in the word 'cow' applies. (*Philosophy of Religion*, p. 19)

The advocates of the ontological argument cheat by slipping 'exists' in amongst the attributes of the idea of God. They try to make 'exists' not only an attribute or predicate of 'God' but a *necessary* predicate, when in fact it is not a predicate at all.

To conclude as I concluded in *How to Be a Philosopher*, as I must always conclude if I am to respect plain logic: If God exists then his existence has to be established by means other than the ontological argument. It is not possible to prove God's existence, or the existence of anything else for that matter, by playing fast and lose with the rules of language and logic.

The refutations offered by Hume, Kant, Russell and Hick completely undermine the ontological argument. As said, the argument does not work. It is an argument that relies on logic that is clearly illogical. This, however, will not prevent religious people who appear at your door, recruiting for their fanatical sect, from offering you the ontological argument as a proof of God's existence. If they do not offer it to you, offer it to them, just to see what reaction you get. It will certainly enliven the debate.

The cosmological argument

The vast, possibly infinite physical universe we inhabit is sometimes called the *cosmos*. The cosmological argument attempts to prove that God exists from the fact that the cosmos exists. There are various forms of the cosmological argument, various cosmological arguments, but they all have in common the attempt to infer God's existence from the existence of the universe as a whole or from the existence of some pervasive feature of the universe.

The cosmological argument, like the teleological argument, is *a posteriori*, which is to say, it is an argument that at least begins with observation and experience of the universe. *A posteriori* means after experience. This sets the cosmological argument radically apart from the ontological argument, which you may recall is *a priori*, depending entirely on pure reason and logic. *A priori* means prior to or apart from experience.

The cosmological argument is older even than the ontological argument, with a history that can be traced back at least as far as the ancient Greeks. In the *Timaeus*, a philosophical dialogue by Plato on the nature of the physical universe, the character, Timaeus of Locri, argues that the origins of the perishable, ever-changing physical world, 'which is always becoming but never in any way is' (*Timaeus*, p. 18), must lie in a perfect, eternal, unchanging metaphysical world. Timaeus holds that because nothing in the physical universe comes into being or changes without a cause then there must be an eternal, metaphysical *demiurge* or God that made the physical universe, a *first cause* of everything that was not itself caused.

> Everything that becomes must do so owing to some cause; for nothing can come to be without a cause ... Let us return, then, and ask the following question about it [the universe]: to which pattern did its constructor work, that which remains the same and unchanging or that which has come to be? If this world here is beautiful and its maker good, clearly he had his eye on the eternal; if the alternative (which it is blasphemy

even to mention) is true, then on something that has come into being. Clearly he had his eye on the eternal: for the world is the fairest of all things that have come into being and he is the best of causes. (*Timaeus*, pp. 18–19)

Amongst his many achievements, Plato founded a school in Athens called the Academy which endured for hundreds of years. Its star pupil was Aristotle, one of Plato's few rivals for the title of greatest Western philosopher ever. Like Plato, Aristotle also explores the cosmological argument in his writings, particularly in his great work, *Physics*. Aristotle rejects the idea of first cause as he thinks that the physical world is eternal and did not have a beginning, but he nonetheless argues that there must be that which is itself unmoving and unchanging that continually moves and animates the physical world. This is the idea of the unmoved mover or prime mover that is so central to the cosmological argument.

As noted earlier, the teachings of Aristotle had a huge influence on medieval theology, particularly the work of the great Catholic theologian, Saint Thomas Aquinas. The best way to start getting to grips with the ins and outs and pros and cons of the cosmological argument is to jump forward in time over 1,500 years from ancient Greece to medieval France and Italy and examine in turn the cosmological arguments of Aquinas as put forward in the first three of his *five ways*, his five proofs of

God's existence as contained in his *Summa Theologiae*. The first three of Aquinas five ways are:

1 The unmoved mover argument, sometimes known as the unchanged changer or prime mover argument.

2 The uncaused causer or first cause argument.

3 The contingency and necessity argument.

The unmoved mover argument

The movement referred to in the unmoved mover argument can be change of place, but what Aquinas principally has in mind, as does Aristotle, is change of state, such as the change of state from ice to water. Central to ancient and medieval physics are the notions of potentiality and actuality. The universe can be seen as a succession of entities that are undergoing or have undergone the actualization of their potential; as a succession of actualized potentials. Ice has the potential to become water, or, as we might say, ice is potential water. Importantly, although ice is potential water, it does not have the capacity to actualize this potential by itself. Its change of state from solid to liquid, from colder to warmer, must be actualized by something that is already actually warm, such as sunlight. The theory is that whatever thing in the universe is moved, as in changed, must be moved by another thing that is already *actually* what the thing to be moved is only *potentially* until such time as it is moved.

So, according to the theory of potentiality and actuality, nothing in the universe changes without being changed by something else. Now, does this imply an *infinite regress* of change? Does it imply that everything that brings about change must itself be the product of change? Aquinas thinks not. He argues that an infinite regress of changes is impossible, as an infinite regress of changes cannot give rise to the phenomenon of change as such. Simply to argue that change is due to prior change *ad infinitum* fails to explain why there is change. The phenomenon of constant change that is observable throughout the universe cannot ultimately give rise to itself, as though it were mysteriously and unaccountably born of infinite regress itself.

As J. L. Mackie argues by analogy in his book, *The Miracle of Theism: Arguments for and against the Existence of God,* a watch without a mainspring cannot achieve motion by having instead an infinite train of gear wheels, just as a train without an engine cannot achieve motion by having instead an infinite number of carriages. As he says:

> If we were told that there was a watch without a mainspring, we would hardly be reassured by the further information that it had, however, an infinite train of gear-wheels. Nor would

we expect a railway train consisting of an infinite number of carriages, the last pulled along by the second last, the second last by the third last, and so on, to get along without an engine. (*The Miracle of Theism*, p. 90)

As an infinite regress of change and movement cannot itself give rise to change and movement there must be an ultimate source of change and movement that is not itself subject to change: an unchanging, unmoved, prime mover. Aquinas identifies the unchanging, unmoved, prime mover as God, and certainly the notion of God as the prime mover is consistent with the description of God we arrived at in the first chapter of this book when we explored the very idea of a supreme being.

It is important to note that the unmoved mover argument is not the first cause argument in disguise, although it may bear certain important similarities to it. Recall that Aristotle rejects the idea of first cause yet holds that there is an unchanging source of all change, something that is the *being of all becoming* that does not itself change. The unmoved mover argument is not that there was an unmoved movement at some time in the past that began the ongoing process of change that we still observe throughout the universe today, but rather that change as such both *implies* an unmoved mover, here and now, and is ultimately *dependent* upon an unmoved mover, here and now. The unmoved mover perpetually or eternally moves the universe without itself being moved.

In Christian theology the central idea is that God, an eternally unchanging changer, constantly sustains the universe of change, a universe that depends entirely upon him and would instantly cease to exist if he ceased to sustain it. It is said that medieval Christian thinkers were inclined to worry not only about the possibility of the universe ending dramatically over a certain period of time in an apocalypse of fire, but also to worry about the possibility of it ceasing to exist instantaneously should the unmoved mover cease to move it. But then what would move him to do so?

The uncaused causer argument

The uncaused causer or first cause argument is the version of the cosmological argument that most people know best. Even people who have never heard the term 'cosmological argument' may well have heard of the first cause argument or even thought of it for themselves while pondering the origins of the universe.

It only takes a brief examination of the physical world around us to see that it is characterized by chains of cause and effect. Very often, to explain something is to say what caused it. The man's death was caused by the ceiling collapsing on his head. The collapse of the ceiling was caused by its structural weakness. The weakness of the ceiling was caused by water damage. The water damage was caused by a leaky pipe, the leaky pipe by a defective joint and so on. In everyday life we only trace chains of cause and effect back as far as is practically useful to diagnose a problem or allocate responsibility. In deciding that it was the sun that caused the colour in his curtains to fade, a man would not normally ponder what caused the sun itself to exist. But it is, of course, possible to trace chains of cause and effect back and back, to ponder what caused the sun to exist and to ponder what caused whatever caused the sun to exist.

As science tells us, every effect has a cause and every cause itself has a cause. And a thing cannot cause itself because it would have to precede itself in order to do so, which is clearly impossible. But can the chains of cause and effect that characterize the physical universe go back and back forever? To argue for an infinite regress of cause and effect raises the same problems identified above during our examination of the unmoved mover argument. The notion of infinite regress cannot itself account for the phenomenon of cause and effect. 'There is cause and effect because there has been an infinite regress of cause and effect' is surely an explanation that would only satisfy a fool.

So, if an infinite regress of cause and effect is impossible, there must have been a first cause, a cause that set the cause and effect universe going that was not itself caused. Not surprisingly, this first cause, this uncaused causer of the universe, Aquinas identifies as God. As we saw in Chapter 1, it is part and parcel of the very idea of God that he must have caused everything without himself having been caused by anything else. Anything less and he would not be worthy of the title.

At the heart of modern physics is the theory of the *big bang*. The theory that the universe exploded into being 14 billion years ago, that it expanded out from a single, infinitesimally small point called a *singularity* and continues to do so. Incidentally, to think that there is a particular place in the universe where the big bang occurred is to suppose that the universe pre-existed the big bang and that the big bang occurred within it and expanded into it. But given that the entire universe grew from the big bang, and that there was no universe before the big bang – not even an infinite void according to physicists – it can be said that the big bang occurred everywhere, as everywhere in the universe is where the big bang occurred when the universe was nothing but the big bang. In fact, the universe is still nothing but the big bang because the big bang is still happening in the sense that the universe is still expanding out from the big bang. Such are the peculiarities of the big bang theory and the difficulties of trying to describe it in ordinary language without resorting to complex mathematical formulae.

What is perhaps most interesting about the big bang is that although physicists are still researching and pondering exactly what the big bang is and exactly what happened during the first few nanoseconds of its occurrence – the Large Hadron Collider near Geneva is key to this research – there is virtually no doubt that the big bang happened. It is an observable feature of the universe that it continues to expand and cosmic microwave background radiation that can only have been caused by the big bang is easily detected. Amazingly, because light travels at the relatively slow speed of 186,000 miles per second, the further away we look, the further back in time we see. Astronomers using the Hubble Space Telescope have observed astronomical phenomena that existed not long after the big bang started with characteristics that clearly show they were produced by the big bang. One ambitious aim of modern astronomy is to make space telescopes so powerful that they will actually be able to see the big bang itself.

What, as philosophers and theologians, are we to make of all this exciting physics? As early as 1951 the Catholic Church began insisting that the scientific evidence for the big bang supports the Judeo-Christian account of creation. The church argues that the big bang theory clearly shows that the physical universe is not eternal, that it had a beginning. The big bang caused the universe, but as the big bang could not have caused itself, it must, they say, have been caused by something eternal, something uncaused, something that transcends the universe, namely God. In an address to the Pontifical Academy of Sciences in 1951, Pope Pius XII said:

It is undeniable that when a mind enlightened and enriched with modern scientific knowledge weighs this problem calmly, it feels drawn to break through the circle of completely independent or autochthonous [original] matter, whether uncreated or self-created, and to ascend to a creating Spirit. With the same clear and critical look with which it examines and passes judgment on facts, it perceives and recognizes the work of creative omnipotence, whose power, set in motion by the mighty *Fiat* pronounced billions of years ago by the Creating Spirit, spread out over the universe, calling into existence with a gesture of generous love matter bursting with energy. In fact, it would seem that present-day science, with one sweeping step back across millions of centuries, has succeeded in bearing witness to that primordial *Fiat lux* [let there be light] uttered at the moment when, along with matter, there burst forth from nothing a sea of light and radiation, while the particles of chemical elements split and formed into millions of galaxies. (*Address of Pope Pius XII to the Pontifical Academy of Sciences*, paragraph 44, 22 November 1951)

Most physicists would certainly not go along with the Catholic explanation of the big bang, or more to the point, see the big bang as any kind of evidence for God's existence. To factor God into the theory, a God of the gaps, would be to resort to what former rock star turned physicist and atheist, Professor Brian Cox, refers to in his TV shows as 'nonsense and woo-woo'. But what, the ordinary person is left asking, caused the big bang if it was not God or some kind of eternal, all powerful force? It is difficult to comprehend exactly what the physicists are saying without the kind of in-depth knowledge of advanced mathematics that few people in the world possess, but their answer appears to be that nothing caused the big bang. There was no time, no place, no reality before the big bang. All this began with the big bang, including the very phenomenon of cause and effect, so to talk of a time before the big bang is simply nonsensical.

If you are dissatisfied with this answer, and do not simply want to put your dissatisfaction down to your own woeful ignorance of quantum physics, you might be tempted to quote William Shakespeare against Stephen Hawking and insist that 'Nothing can come of nothing' (*King Lear*, Act 1, Scene 1, Quarto Text).

Interestingly, some physicists themselves seem to feel the common sense of old Lear's Parmenidean maxim, as scientific theories of the beginning of the universe are emerging that do at least seem to hint at something perfect, uncaused and eternal that pre-existed the big bang and from which the physical universe somehow arose. We should not, however, confuse what these theories have in mind with what most religious people understand by God. There is no suggestion in these theories of a conscious, personal, moral supreme being. One theory is that not God but the mathematical laws of physics pre-existed the physical universe itself. The theory claims that what is eternal and uncaused is mathematical principles, and that the physical universe is a kind of expression or playing out of the possibilities of mathematics.

This theory is not a million miles from Plato's *theory of forms*, an idealist, anti-materialist theory which argues that the physical universe of particular things is, so to speak, a mere shadow cast by a higher, metaphysical world of perfect, timeless, universal forms, essences or Ideas. For Plato, as for one of his major influences, Pythagoras, the study of mathematics in particular reveals a world of eternal truths of a distinctly higher order of reality than the shifting, changing, cause and effect physical world we encounter through our senses.

Behind the seemingly successful quest for the holy grail of particle physics, the Higgs boson or *God particle* said to be responsible for mass, is the theory that the physical universe is a kind of ongoing asymmetry or disharmony between matter and anti-matter. Not least, there is more matter than anti-matter. This asymmetry began with the big bang. The big bang did not cause this asymmetry, the big bang was itself the start of this asymmetry. Prior to this asymmetry there was perfect symmetry, perfect balance and harmony between all physical forces, or what became physical forces during the big bang. Such was the perfection and purity of this non-state that nothing really existed because all 'forces' entirely cancelled one another out.

Like the previous theories, this theory also appears to postulate that a state of non-physical perfection pre-existed the physical universe. In this theory, however, the suggestion is that the physical universe, as an asymmetry or disharmony, began as the *termination* of a state of perfection, rather than as the *product* of a state of perfection.

Perhaps what there was prior to the big bang was not nothing but a state of pure *being*. It existed but it was utterly without characteristics or determining features. It was not temporal or spatial and had no regions or parts. It was entirely *undifferentiated*. It was not unlike what the existentialist philosopher, Jean-Paul Sartre, calls *being-in-itself*. Being so devoid of determining features that it is indistinguishable from nothingness or non-being, except that, as Sartre says, 'being *is* and nothingness is *not*' (*Being and Nothingness*, p. 39).

Arguably, the big bang was not the beginning of being but the beginning of nothingness, the beginning of there being both being and nothingness. It was the occurrence of nothingness, as the non-being or negation of being, that gave rise to the physical universe as a process of becoming and change, that gave rise to the dance between being and nothingness that is the daily reality we all experience. Without nothingness or non-being, being has no possibilities or characteristics, it just *is*.

Non-being gives rise to time, for example, by allowing there to be *no longer* and *not yet*. Non-being, so to speak, loosens up pure undifferentiated being by introducing differences, distinctions and distances into it. This is *not* that, here is *not* there, then is *not* now and so on. It is non-being or lack that makes our diverse, differentiated, spatial, temporal universe of distinct phenomena possible. Such a universe requires non-being or lack every bit as much as it requires being. Many great thinkers in the long history of philosophy, from Heraclitus and Spinoza to Hegel and Sartre, have noted that *omnis determinatio est negatio* – everything is determined by non-being or negation.

Now, why the state of perfection or pure being terminated, why nothingness arose to produce the physical universe through its relationship with being, why something happened that threw a perfect harmony devoid of all physical qualities into the disharmony of the physical, how a fly happened in the purest of pure ointments so as to taint the whole with physical existence, what precipitated the 'malady of being' (*Being and Nothingness*, p. 641), I have absolutely no idea!

Even though nothingness, as the non-being of being, is dependent upon being, it cannot be said that being actively gave rise to nothingness. Being-in-itself, in simply being what it is, has no possibilities. All possibility arises in and through non-being. So there could have been no *capacity* within being-in-itself to give rise to non-being. Yet 14 billion years ago non-being arose from being to haunt being and the physical universe began. Mystery. Seemingly, whatever hypotheses philosophers formulate to try and explain why this absolute event occurred will remain hypotheses because there can be no final validation or invalidation of them. Perhaps the physicists can do better, but surely even physicists cannot surmount *logical* barriers to knowledge and verify the unverifiable.

Physics, of course, is a science, so it is not actually in the business of speculating that there was or was not a certain kind of being before the big bang. Physicists can only speak as their mathematically based theories and observational findings dictate, which at the moment do not really take them beyond the big bang.

Whatever physicists say, an ordinary person, or even a philosopher, will probably refuse to accept that it is possible for something to arise from *absolutely* nothing, and hence be inclined to argue that there must be that which is eternal and necessary, even if it is not God as generally understood.

Talk of that which is necessary brings us neatly to a consideration of the third of Aquinas' five ways.

The contingency and necessity argument

The astute reader will recall that we touched upon this argument in Chapter 1 while considering the notion that God is necessary and self-sufficient whereas the universe is not. There we noted that 'contingent' means 'unnecessary' or 'need not be'.

The argument goes: everything in the universe is contingent, it need not be and once was not. You need not be, indeed the entire human race need not be. Even the sun and the stars need not be. None of these things existed once and one day they will no longer exist. They just happen to exist at the moment. Now, if everything once was not then once there was nothing. And if once there was nothing there would be nothing now because as Parmenides says, 'Nothing comes from nothing.' But, of course, there is not nothing, there is the very real physical universe we observe all around us. There must, therefore, be something that is not contingent, something necessary that gave rise to the universe of contingent things. Simply put, there must be something that must be in order for there to be things that need not be. All things cannot be contingent.

Once again, the argument hinges upon the impossibility of an infinite regress. The universe is a process of contingent things giving rise to further contingent things, a process of contingent things forming and passing away. To claim, however, that this process goes back *ad infinitum* fails to explain how there is a sequence of contingent things. Suppose, in an attempt to be rid of the problem of infinite regress, a person claimed that there was a first contingent thing that gave rise to all subsequent contingent things. This would amount to saying either that the first contingent thing caused itself, which is impossible as it would have to pre-exist itself in order to do so, or that the first contingent thing was in fact not contingent but necessary. That it was, or rather is, a being that must be and cannot not be.

Here is the crux of the cosmological argument. However you try to reason about the existence of the contingent universe as such, eventually, if you are to avoid a confused or nonsensical assertion, you will come around to the conclusion that there must be something that is not contingent but necessary, something that does not depend upon anything else for its existence. Aquinas, of course, like all religious thinkers, equates this necessary being with God.

It is important to distinguish the meaning of the term 'necessary being' as used in the context of the cosmological argument from the meaning of the term as used in the context of the ontological argument. The ontological argument refers to a being that is *logically* necessary, a being that it would be a logical contradiction to deny the existence of, a being that cannot be thought of as not existing. For its part, the cosmological argument refers to a being that is *factually* necessary, a being that it would not be a logical contradiction to deny the existence of, a being that can be thought of as not existing, but nonetheless must exist if the contingent universe is to be accounted for.

If trying to get your brain around such a subtle distinction makes your head spin, then simply recall that the ontological argument is a purely *a priori* argument that attempts to prove the existence of God from the very idea of God, whereas the cosmological argument is an *a posteriori* argument that attempts to prove the existence of God from the existence of the universe.

Now, as was said above while we were reflecting on the science of physics, not all thinkers who agree that there must be something that is necessary, eternal and unmoved, think, as Aquinas does, that this being must also be conscious, personal and moral; that it must be *God* in the full-blown, religious sense of the word. That which is necessary might be a blind, non-conscious and therefore impersonal and amoral force, a pure law or principle of physics, amounting to nothing more than something that can be described mathematically.

Against this atheistic view, religious thinkers will argue that we need to look at what has sprung from that which is necessary, namely a universe with a coherent structure that contains complexity, beauty, meaning, value and so on. In their view, this indicates that that which is necessary must be infinitely more than a blind, proto-physical force. If it is capable of giving rise to the wonders of the universe, then perfect power, perfect intelligence, perfect creativity and even perfect goodness must be aspects of its necessary and eternal being. Such arguments take us away from the territory of the cosmological argument into that of the teleological argument which we will examine in detail in due course.

The cosmological argument has been reformulated and criticized repeatedly since the time of Aquinas. One of the best known reformulations is found in the writings of the seventeenth-century German rationalist, Gottfried Wilhelm Leibniz. Leibniz was a polymath, which means he was an expert in every major intellectual discipline of his day. He is best known now as a philosopher, but as well as writing on such topics as history, politics and medicine, he was an outstanding mathematician and scientist. He invented calculus, a key branch of mathematics, around the same time as Isaac Newton and there remains a huge controversy as to who really thought of it first. With his fingers in so many pies it is not surprising that Leibniz has been called 'the Aristotle of the modern era' – if you call the seventeenth century modern. Given the long history of philosophy, it *is* relatively recent.

Like all proponents of the cosmological argument, Leibniz argues that the universe cannot be accounted for by an appeal to infinite regress, although it is the regress of *explanations* rather than the regress of *events* that he focuses on. The universe may or may not have always existed, either way, there is nothing about it or within it to explain *why* it exists. Leibniz argues that whether or not it is known, there is always an explanation for everything, a reason for every truth. This is known as the *principle of sufficient reason*. In Leibniz's view, the principle of sufficient reason dictates that because the reason for the existence of the universe cannot be found within the universe then it must lie outside of it. There must be some being that is the reason for the existence of the universe, a being that needs no further reason to exist. You will probably not be surprised to learn that Leibniz considers this entirely self-sufficient being to be God.

Leibniz also uses an argument that is closely related to the one above, an argument the general form of which should be quite familiar to you by now given everything that has already been said. This is his *argumentum a contingentia mundi,* his *argument from the contingency of the universe.* He argues that the existence of the universe is a contingent fact, that its existence is not necessary. Therefore, the reason for the existence of the universe must lie outside of the universe in something that is not contingent but necessary.

Leibniz sums up his position, and the cosmological argument generally, in his *Principles of Nature and of Grace, Founded on Reason,* published in 1714. Note that in amongst his talk of contingency, necessity and sufficient reason there is also a version of the unmoved mover argument:

Now this sufficient reason of the existence of the universe cannot be found in the series of contingent things, that is to say, of bodies and of their representations in souls [objects and ideas]. For since matter is in itself indifferent to motion or to rest, and to one motion rather than another, it cannot itself contain the reason of motion, still less of a particular motion. And although the present motion which is in matter arises from the one before it, and this in its turn from the one before that, we are no further on however far we go; for the same question always remains. Thus the sufficient reason, which needs no further reason, must be outside this series of contingent things, and must lie in a substance which is the cause of this series, or which is a necessary being, bearing the reason of its existence within itself; otherwise we should still not have a sufficient reason, with which we could stop. And this final reason of things is called *God.* (*Principles of Nature and of Grace, Founded on Reason,* in *Leibniz: Philosophical Writings,* p. 199)

Why the cosmological argument fails

Having set out the cosmological argument in some detail, it is time now to consider objections to it, for it is an argument that has been much molested by critics, certainly since the time of Leibniz, who was just about the last major philosopher to give it his unqualified support.

It is a widely held view in modern philosophy that the cosmological argument is outdated, that it relies on a mixture of discredited ancient and medieval physics and fundamentally flawed metaphysics – metaphysics being the use of concepts that belong rightfully to empirical experience in an illegitimate attempt to exceed the bounds of empirical experience and reason about what lies beyond the physical. The general idea is that the metaphysical reasoning involved in the cosmological argument is fundamentally flawed because *all* metaphysical reasoning is fundamentally flawed.

I will return to the whole issue of metaphysics shortly, after considering various other objections that have been raised against the cosmological argument. These objections do not necessarily totally undermine the cosmological argument, but they nonetheless chip away at its credibility rendering it far less than the *proof* of God's existence some philosophers have claimed it to be; they reduce it, at best, to a set of questionable *hypotheses* about the origins of the physical universe.

It is worth beginning with an objection that has actually already been raised. There may be a necessary being, but it does not follow that it is anything like God as generally understood. It may be mathematical principles or pure energy rather than a conscious, personal, moral being. Philosophers like Aquinas use the cosmological argument to *reinforce* a belief in a conscious, personal, moral God that they hold on other grounds – faith, Scripture and so on. There is nothing in the cosmological argument itself that produces the unavoidable conclusion that what is necessary, uncaused and unmoved is a sentient being.

Secondly, modern physics rejects as simply incorrect the Aristotelian notions of potentiality and actuality that are so central to the unmoved mover argument. It is simply not the case that actual x must be caused by that which is already actual x. One simple piece of empirical evidence to support this claim is that two cold objects rubbed together produce heat.

Thirdly, the contingency and necessity argument may be wrong to assert that the physical universe is contingent. Although the argument is right that the more obvious objects in the universe are contingent, that everything from pencils to planets comes into and goes out of existence, it does not follow that the basic building blocks of objects are contingent. Atoms can be split but the matter and energy of which they are made, the sub-atomic particles and forces, so scientists tells us, cannot be destroyed.

Against the cosmological argument, it can be conjectured that what is necessary and eternal is not a supreme metaphysical being outside the universe that caused the universe and perpetually sustains it in its apparent contingency, but the basic fabric of the universe itself, matter and energy. Arguably, the universe is a brute fact, it was never caused, it just is. It cannot be explained by something beyond it and does not need to be explained by something beyond it. It follows from this that anything approaching an ultimate explanation of existence can only come from physics.

Just as this line of reasoning is about to concede everything to physics, however, physics itself raises a problem in the form of the big bang theory. In claiming that the universe had a beginning, the big bang theory seems to suggest that matter and energy are not eternal. One way out of this problem is to argue that the universe is oscillating, that the same eternal matter and energy expands and contracts eternally. The big bang was not an absolute beginning, only the beginning of this present universe, an event that followed immediately from the big crunch of the previous universe.

Unfortunately for the oscillating universe theory, though it has the advantage of reinforcing the view that matter and energy are eternal and necessary, the weight of empirical evidence seems to be against it. Physicists tell us that the expansion of the universe is speeding up, that the spread of matter and energy over an ever increasing area means that it is highly unlikely the force of gravity will ever be able to crunch it all back together again.

There may, of course, be another force that physicists are presently unaware of that has the power to crunch the universe, but at the moment the smart money is on the universe expanding forever, spreading its energy so thinly that it will eventually undergo what is called *heat death*. It will still exist, but there will be insufficient energy in any one place for anything to happen. Physicists certainly need to be careful here not to suggest that the universe ends completely, for anything that can end is contingent and must, so the argument goes, have been ultimately caused by something that is necessary.

Fourthly, it can be asked why there must be a single activation of causes? There might be several independent uncaused causes, a whole multiplicity of them rather than one supreme first cause. This argument denies the existence of a supreme being in so far as a supreme being must be the first cause of every other cause in order to be supreme. This argument could be taken to suggest a pantheon of gods, each of them necessary and uncaused, but it rules out the single supreme being of the Judeo-Christian tradition.

Lastly, it can be argued that God created the universe but now he no longer exists. Perhaps he ceased to exist the moment the universe was created. Maybe the cosmological argument can only suggest that there *was* a God, not that there is a God now. This god would not, of course, be worthy of the title *supreme being*, even though he had the power to create the universe, as a god that ceases to exist is not something than which nothing greater can be thought.

So much for arguments that chip away at the credibility of the cosmological argument. The real problem with the cosmological argument is not that it can be weakened by throwing various objections and reservations against it, but that it is ultimately nonsensical, as, arguably, is all metaphysical reasoning, all reasoning that undertakes to speculate about what lies beyond sensory, empirical experience.

The great Scottish empiricist philosopher, David Hume, whose canny, no nonsense approach to philosophy has helped generations of thinkers out of many a jam, was among the first philosophers to argue that all metaphysical reasoning, for all its profundity, complexity and tradition, is nothing but a tangle of confused, empty and futile speculations leading to so-called conclusions that it is impossible to ever verify as true or false. Metaphysics, for Hume, is characterized by an objectionable obscurity that is not only 'painful and fatiguing' but 'the inevitable source of uncertainty and error' (*Enquiries Concerning Human Understanding*, p. 11). He goes on to say:

> Here indeed lies the justest and most plausible objection against a considerable part of metaphysics, that they are not properly a science; but arise either from the fruitless efforts of human vanity, which would penetrate into subjects utterly inaccessible to the understanding, or from the craft of popular superstitions, which, being unable to defend themselves on fair ground, raise these intangling brambles to cover and protect their weakness. Chaced from the open country, these robbers fly into the forest, and lie in wait to break in upon every unguarded avenue of the mind, and overwhelm it with religious fears and prejudices. (*Enquiries Concerning Human Understanding*, p. 11)

Hume was of the firm opinion that all understanding is based on empirical experience and therefore limited to empirical experience. We can only know what our senses tell us, and whatever theories and hypotheses we may come up with about the nature of reality can only ever be validated or invalidated by our empirical experience of reality.

For example, if John claims that every event has a cause, Jane can look at the world to see if John's claim is true or not. She can test John's theory against the evidence of her senses and reach a reasonably meaningful, useful and satisfactory conclusion about the nature of reality. However, if John decides to indulge in metaphysics, to raise 'intangling brambles' by arguing that the universe has a cause that transcends it, a cause utterly beyond what it is possible for Jane or anyone else to experience, Jane clearly cannot test John's theory against the evidence of the senses. And if the evidence of the senses is, in the end, the only means of deciding what is true or false, then it is *impossible* for anyone to know whether or not the universe has a transcendent cause.

In a section in his *Critique of Pure Reason* titled 'The Impossibility of a Cosmological Proof of the Existence of God' (*Critique of Pure Reason*, pp. 507–14), Kant argues that to talk about the universe as a whole as having been caused is to misapply the concept of causation by using it outside of its proper, empirical context. The concept of causation belongs exclusively to our experience of what Kant calls the *sensible world* and applies meaningfully only to our experience of the sensible world, yet the cosmological argument attempts to utilize the concept of causation to extend our knowledge beyond the sensible world. The use of the concept of causation in the cosmological argument is a true fish out of water. As Kant says:

> The principle of causality has no meaning and no criterion for its application save only in the sensible world. But in the cosmological proof it is precisely in order to enable us to advance beyond the sensible world that it is employed. (*Critique of Pure Reason*, p. 511)

To speculate that the universe has a transcendent cause, let alone a cause in the form of a necessary, unmoved, sentient, supreme being, may be entertaining and thought provoking for those of us who enjoy such things – even Hume doubtless enjoyed indulging in idle metaphysical speculation from time to time – but it is nonetheless, as Hume and his generations of disciples are keen to point out, an ultimately futile exercise. Such metaphysical speculation can never get beyond being mere speculation, it can never reach a clear, truly satisfactory conclusion. The only real point to indulging in metaphysical speculation is to learn, through one's own experience of the exercise, just how ultimately futile and fruitless metaphysical speculation really is. Whatever metaphysical speculation seems to imply can only ever be taken as 'certain' on the grounds of faith or bias and never on the grounds of plain reason and philosophy.

Hume was the forefather of a twentieth-century philosophical movement called *logical positivism*. The logical positivists were particularly influenced by a principle that has come to be known as *Hume's fork*. It led them to establish their own very similar principle known as the *principle of verification*. Both principles state that only propositions that it is possible to verify as true or false are meaningful. Propositions that cannot possibly be verified as true or false are, logically speaking, meaningless, even if they are superficially meaningful on a grammatical level. Hume argues that there are only two types of proposition that can be verified as true or false, therefore only two types of proposition that are meaningful. He refers to these two types of proposition as *relations of ideas* and *matters of fact*.

Relations of ideas refers to all the purely logical relationships that are found, for example, in mathematics. The proposition 'A father is a male parent' expresses a relation of ideas. Once a person has learnt what the terms 'father' and 'male parent' mean, the truth of the proposition 'A father is a male parent' is unavoidable. Hume's *relations of ideas* are today called *analytic propositions*. Such propositions simply exhibit logic rather than any kind of metaphysical knowledge. They do not tell us anything about the world, and certainly nothing about metaphysical worlds beyond the senses. They are entirely self-referential.

Matters of fact include all those propositions that are held to be true (or false) on the basis of the evidence of present or past sensory experience. 'Trees have leaves', 'The sun is round', 'Paris is the capital of France' and so on. Hume's *matters of fact* are today called *synthetic propositions*. Most of our talking and thinking is made up of synthetic propositions.

Where is all this leading, I hear you cry. Have our brain cells not suffered enough during this long, arduous section on the cosmological argument? Well, the point is that the metaphysical propositions that comprise the greater part of the cosmological argument or arguments – propositions referring to an unmoved mover, a first cause, a necessary being and so on – are neither relations of ideas or matters of fact, neither purely logical or purely scientific.

The cosmological argument is not a purely logical argument because, as was said at the very start of this section, it is an *a posteriori* argument that at least begins with observation and experience of the universe, even if it does not remain within the bounds of observation and experience. And the fact that it does not remain within empirical bounds, but instead takes off from its empirical launch pad into heady realms of metaphysical speculation, clearly reveals that it is not a purely scientific argument.

So, by the standards of Hume's fork and the principle of verification, the cosmological argument is neither true or false, neither right or wrong, but simply meaningless and nonsensical. As it is neither a purely logical or a purely empirical argument, its metaphysical cosmological assertions cannot be verified as true or false by either of the only two means of verifying anything as true or false, namely logic and science. Like all metaphysical reasoning, it is, as the logical positivists say, *unverifiable*, and ought therefore to be, as Hume says, committed to the flames 'for it can contain nothing but sophistry and illusion' (*Enquiries Concerning Human Understanding,* p. 165). A philosophically appropriate but nonetheless sad end for such an ancient, illustrious and alluring argument.

The teleological argument

In *The Hitchhiker's Guide to the Galaxy*, a brilliant fusion of philosophy, science-fiction and comedy, Douglas Adams tells the tale of the legendary Babel fish, 'probably the oddest thing in the universe' (*The Hitchhiker's Guide to the Galaxy,* p. 52). The Babel fish is small and yellow and feeds on brainwave energy. It nourishes itself with unconscious mental frequencies and excretes conscious frequencies along with speech centre nerve signals. The result is that when a person places a Babel fish in his ear he can instantly understand any language in the universe. By removing all communication barriers between different peoples the poor Babel fish has caused more wars than anything else that has ever existed.

Now, the Babel fish is so strange and so useful that anyone might be forgiven for thinking that it could not have come about by chance, that it must have been created by God, and that God, therefore, must exist. Always one step ahead of his reader, however, Adams actually jokes that the Babel fish is a 'final and clinching proof of the non-existence of God' (*The Hitchhiker's Guide to the Galaxy,* p. 52).

He argues that the proof of God's existence that the Babel fish provides denies the all important faith without which God is, in his own words, nothing. (Outside the context of Adams' imagination, God never actually said, 'Without faith I am nothing', or at least, it is not a quote from the Bible.) Adams has Man say to God, 'But … the Babel fish is a dead giveaway isn't it? It could not have evolved by chance. It proves you exist, and so therefore, by your own arguments, you don't. QED' (*The Hitchhiker's Guide to the Galaxy,* p. 52). In a catastrophic failure of omniscience, God admits to not having thought of this argument and 'promptly vanishes in a puff of logic' (*The Hitchhiker's Guide to the Galaxy,* p. 52).

Had Adams argued, as it appears he is about to argue, that the extreme unlikelihood of the Babel fish having evolved by chance means that it must have been created by God, then Adams would have employed the teleological argument. Instead, he sets the teleological argument up, only to knock it down at the last moment with an argument that is 'a load of dingo's kidneys' according to 'most leading theologians' (*The Hitchhiker's Guide to the Galaxy*, p. 52).

The Babel fish story is so entertaining that I can never resist using it as a way of introducing the teleological argument, even if having to also explain Adams' crazy counter-argument runs the risk of causing temporary confusion. If you were slightly confused, even for a moment, then spare a thought for one or two less able students I have taught over the years. Not only were they totally bamboozled by the twists and turns of Adam's pseudo-argument, and unable to see the teleological argument in amongst all the humour and irony, they thought that the Babel fish actually exists or, at least, that I was teaching that it actually exists. Perhaps I am the fool and the last laugh is on me because maybe the Babel fish does actually exist somewhere in the infinite universe.

The teleological argument is just about everyone's favourite argument for the existence of God. Sir David Attenborough shows his captivated audience an insect that camouflages itself by looking exactly like a stick, or a deep-sea fish that has a glowing protrusion to attract prey, or a chameleon that can change colour to match any background, and not surprisingly many people conclude that these extraordinary creatures cannot have come about by accident. Indeed, even the humblest creature, a woodlouse for example, is so exquisitely complex that to many people the suggestion that a mere combination of chance and blind natural processes gave rise to the creature sounds ridiculous.

The woodlouse is a part of nature, and nature as a whole is so diverse, so intricate, so ordered, so balanced, so beautiful, so awesome, that it must surely have been designed and created by a supremely intelligent, all powerful, omnificent being, namely God. How does a spider know how to spin a web? Answer: God. Why does a giraffe have a neck long enough to allow it to reach high leaves? Answer: God.

It is not only in the living world that the many advocates of the teleological argument see God's handiwork. God placed the Earth just the right distance from the sun, in the so-called Goldilocks zone, not too hot and not too cold. Any nearer and it would have fried like Venus, any further away and it would have frozen like Mars. Even the gas giant Jupiter can be seen as part of God's big plan because its huge gravitational field sucks in many asteroids that would otherwise plough into the Earth.

You get the picture because, on a basic level at least, you are already very familiar with the teleological argument. Unlike the ontological argument, and perhaps even the cosmological argument, it is a part of everyday life. A person does not have to be religious to refer to the wonders of the universe as *creation*, and we even hear scientists and naturalists like David Attenborough refer to the *design* of a bird's wing. We even sing about the teleological argument:

All things bright and beautiful,

All creatures great and small,

All things wise and wonderful,

The Lord God made them all.

Each little flower that opens,

Each little bird that sings,

He made their glowing colours,

He made their tiny wings.

('All Things Bright and Beautiful', verses 1 and 2, *Hymns Ancient and Modern*)

So much for the playschool version of the teleological argument or argument from design. We need now to explore the teleological argument in its *philosophical* detail, discover something of its history and discover why, indeed, it is called the *teleological argument*. Not least, we need to discover what is wrong with it.

Aristotle to Paley – the history of the teleological argument

Like the cosmological argument, the teleological argument is *a posteriori*, an argument that begins with observation and experience of the universe. *A posteriori* means after experience. This sets the teleological argument apart from the ontological argument, which is *a priori*, depending entirely on pure reason and logic. *A priori* means prior to or apart from experience.

The word 'teleological' derives from the Greek word *telos* which means *end*, *goal* or *purpose*. The *telos* of a thing is the end goal at which it aims. Aristotle is a teleologist who argues that everything in nature has an end goal or purpose proper to it. We understand what things are by understanding the end goal at which they aim. Aristotle makes this one of the central principles of both his biology and his ethics. We understand an acorn, for example, as that which is *meant* to become an oak tree, and an acorn fully achieves its end goal if indeed it becomes a healthy, reproductive oak. An acorn that fails to become a healthy oak fails to achieve its *telos*. Its failure to achieve its *telos* is likely to be due to its serving the purposes of another being with its own *telos*. It might be eaten by a pig, for example.

Anything that achieves its proper end goal is said to *flourish*. Aristotle is particularly interested in human flourishing, in identifying the proper end goal of human existence. He argues that the goal of human existence is the achievement of true happiness or *eudaimonia*, the achievement of a full and balanced life governed by moderation and wisdom.

The key idea to be drawn from Aristotle's teleology, as far as the teleological argument for the existence of God is concerned, is his view that all of nature exhibits *purposiveness*, which the dictionary defines as 'relating to, having, or indicating conscious intention'. The million dollar question to keep in mind is, where does this real or apparent purposiveness of nature come from?

We have already seen how influential the ideas of Aristotle and other ancient Greek philosophers were on subsequent thinkers, and there are certainly clear echoes of the ancient Greek notion of teleology in the writings of many later philosophers, particularly those of the Roman and medieval periods. In his philosophical dialogue, *The Nature of the Gods* (*De natura deorum*), the Roman politician and philosopher, Marcus Tullius Cicero, considers the theological positions of different schools of philosophy. Speaking for the Stoics, the character Balbus says:

> But when we Stoics say that the universe both coheres and is ordered by the work of nature, we do not regard it as being like a clod of earth, or a pebble, or something of that kind which lacks organic unity, but rather to be like a tree or a living creature which does not present a haphazard appearance, but bears clear evidence of order and similarity to human design. (*The Nature of the Gods*, Book 2, para. 82, p. 76)

Moving on from the Romans, we come once again to the greatest of the medieval Aristotelian philosophers, our old friend, Saint Thomas Aquinas. Aquinas makes the teleological argument the fifth of his five ways, arguing that the self-evident order, harmony and regularity of nature indicates *guidedness* or *governance*, indicates the workings of a supremely intelligent guiding, governing force. Echoing his own guiding light, Aristotle, Aquinas notes that nature is teleological, that there is an order of actions towards an end goal in all things that obey natural laws, even when these things lack awareness. 'This is clear,' he says, 'from the fact that they always, or usually, act in the same way so as to achieve what is best (and therefore reach their goal by purpose, not by chance)' (*Summa Theologiae*, p. 26). Nothing that lacks awareness, however, can tend towards a goal except under the direction of something with awareness and understanding. The *telos* of an arrow, for example, is to hit a target, but as an arrow has no awareness, it requires an archer to direct it to the target. Aquinas concludes:

> But things lacking intelligence tend to a goal only as directed by one with knowledge and understanding. Arrows, for instance, need archers. So, there is a being with intelligence who directs all natural things to ends, we call this being 'God'. (*Summa Theologiae*, p. 26)

The best-known exponent of the teleological argument in somewhat more recent times is the English philosopher and theologian, William Paley. Born in 1743, Paley taught philosophy at Cambridge before entering the clergy and becoming Archdeacon of Carlisle. An exceptional scholar, Paley strove to be familiar with the latest developments in philosophy, ethics, law, politics and science. He sought to square the cutting-edge ideas of his day, particularly scientific ideas and discoveries, with his own traditional Christian views and values, and for this reason has often been described as a Christian apologist.

This said, it is a fair criticism of Paley that in defending the teleological argument in his major work, *Natural Theology*, published in 1802, he largely ignored the devastating criticisms of the argument made by David Hume only twenty-three years earlier in his groundbreaking, *Dialogues Concerning Natural Religion*, an extremely controversial and irreligious book for its time. The book was published in 1779, three years after Hume's death. Even he did not dare publish it in his lifetime, and during the twenty-five years he spent polishing the text friends often advised him to destroy it for his own safety.

Historians tend to agree that although Paley was aware of Hume's criticisms, he failed, like most of the academic establishment of his time, to absorb their full impact into his own thinking. Largely because of his lifelong opposition to religion, Hume had been an establishment outsider. This meant that his philosophy took a long time to come to prominence, and certainly at the time Paley wrote *Natural Theology* Hume was not widely read or discussed. Arguably, Hume was just too cutting-edge even for a would-be progressive like Paley, whose ship would probably have sunk before it set sail had he tried to take Hume's ideas fully on board.

As a man of science as well as philosophy and religion, Paley takes the scientific discoveries of his day, particularly new insights into the wonders of human anatomy, as clear evidence for intelligent design. Like many thinkers before him, Cicero for example, Paley views the universe as a vast, well ordered mechanism, and living things in particular as intrinsic parts of that mechanism, encapsulating the subtlety and complexity of the whole and indicative of clear deliberation and intention behind the whole.

To make his point, Paley compares the world to a watch and God to a watchmaker. This analogy was widely used before Paley, but Paley certainly made it his own. It is the watchmaker analogy for which Paley is now most famous, indeed his name has become almost synonymous with it.

Paley imagines that while crossing a heath he pitches his foot against a stone and wonders how the stone came to be there. He says he might possibly answer, for all he knows to the contrary, that the stone has lain there forever. It is clear that Paley does not actually think the stone has lain there forever – he would have known something of the emerging science of geology – but he argues that the absurdity of the claim that the stone has lain there forever is not easily shown and that anyone might be forgiven for supposing that it has.

Now, if someone finds a *watch* upon the heath it is inconceivable that they could draw the conclusion that it has lain there forever. They could not draw such a conclusion as they would clearly discover in the watch what they could not discover in the stone: 'that its several parts are framed and put together for a purpose, e.g. that they are so formed and adjusted as to produce motion, and that motion so regulated as to point out the hour of the day' (*Natural Theology*, p. 7).

Paley continues for several pages beautifully extending and embroidering his watch example. He comments on how the spring of the watch is made of steel, a metal which is sufficiently elastic to serve as a spring, while the gear wheels are made of brass to keep them from rusting. He even ponders what a person would think if they discovered that the watch had the complex wherewithal to reproduce itself in a manner comparable to animal reproduction, 'a mould for instance, or a complex adjustment of laths, files, and other tools' (*Natural Theology*, p. 11). This discovery would not only 'increase his admiration of the contrivance' (*Natural Theology*, p. 11), it would reinforce the conclusion he soon reached on finding the watch, that its construction was the result of deliberate design and supreme artistry.

Given all that has been said so far, the point that Paley is seeking to make with his analogy is clear: If a man who discovers a watch with all its intricacies is obliged to conclude that the watch must have an intelligent and skilful maker, then a man discovering living nature – a phenomenon so intricate in form and function that a mere watch is a crude contraption by comparison – is all the more obliged to conclude that living nature must have a *supremely* intelligent and skilful creator, a divine watchmaker.

Why the teleological argument fails

The teleological argument is a reasonable argument to which many people the world over still subscribe. It is what philosophers call a *tenable* argument, an argument that can, as we have seen, be upheld, believed, maintained and defended by sane, intelligent people such as Cicero, Aquinas and Paley. But it is nonetheless a flawed argument, even if, as with the other theistic arguments, its flaws are not nearly so obvious as the apparent but illusory rightness of the argument itself.

Not only is the teleological argument flawed in various ways, when it comes to accounting for the diversity and complexity of life on Earth there is a powerful scientific alternative to the teleological argument that threatens to make the teleological argument redundant, if indeed it has not done so already. That alternative is Charles Darwin's theory of evolution by means of natural selection, which requires no notion of a divine watchmaker, or indeed any watchmaker at all. More on the theory of evolution as we move forward.

As mentioned, David Hume had already subjected the teleological argument to a series of devastating criticisms in his *Dialogues Concerning Natural Religion* some years before Paley published his *Natural Theology*, but it was not until Hume's ideas came to prominence towards the middle of the nineteenth century that his criticisms really took their toll. Hume's *Dialogues Concerning Natural Religion* are now generally accepted as providing the classic critique of the teleological or design argument.

Dialogues Concerning Natural Religion is a philosophical conversation or *dialogue* between three characters, Cleanthes, Philo and Demea, narrated by a fourth character, Pamphilus. The dialogue form has a long and noble history in philosophy dating back to the ancient Greeks. Most notably, the entire works of Plato are written in dialogue. As philosophical ideas are often best developed and refined through debate, the dialogue form easily lends itself to philosophical writing and can be a better and more balanced way of exploring opposing viewpoints than a straightforward 'one voice' exposition.

Using dialogue allowed Hume to put his own radical views across without them appearing as too obviously *his* views. They appear as part of an ongoing discussion between three fictitious characters rather than Hume's own forthright and settled opinions. Arguably, it was not predominantly caution in face of the church that led Hume to adopt this approach – it was after all his express wish that he be long dead before the book was published – but his belief that a balanced debate was more likely to make headway in the conservative and Christian world of academia than an overt and blasphemous polemic.

The book is nonetheless polemical because, although it pays lip service to religious orthodoxy, it subjects the traditional arguments for God's existence to the kind of withering criticism that nobody had really dared to set down in writing before. It is careful to insist that God exists – all the speakers insist that God exists – while putting forward a series of arguments claiming that philosophy and theology cannot prove God's existence or discover anything about his nature.

One of Hume's main criticisms of the teleological argument is that the widely used machine or artefact analogy is weak and confused whether it is applied to parts of the universe such as living organisms or to the universe as a whole. Living organisms and machines are very different. Machines are deliberately designed and individually assembled from a collection of components, whereas living organisms are never assembled but grow by means of cell division and are always part of the ongoing life of a species.

Machines and artefacts do not grow and change of themselves as living organisms do, and can only grow and change if deliberately enlarged or altered by an artisan. Living organisms are a single unified whole, even if it often suits the aims of science and medicine to perceive and treat the whole as an assemblage of parts. A living organism is not manufactured as a watch is manufactured and to describe any form of organic reproduction and growth as *manufacture* is misplaced. Human beings, for example, are not manufactured by their parents and nobody but Frankenstein's monster would claim to have been manufactured.

As for the analogy between a machine and the universe as a whole, the complexity of a machine must be understood as resulting from the deliberate assemblage of components by an engineer, whereas the complexity of the universe can be understood as resulting from, and is most usefully explained by, the action of non-deliberate natural forces and processes – physical, chemical and biological.

Except for human and perhaps some animal constructions, the structures of the universe *evolved*, they were never built. Also, machines are precisely not organic – otherwise they would be living organisms and not machines – whereas the universe is partly organic, in which case it might be better compared to a potato than a watch. As Hume says: 'And does not a plant or an animal, which springs from vegetation or generation, bear a stronger resemblance to the world, than does any artificial machine, which arises from reason and design?' (*Dialogues Concerning Natural Religion*, pp. 87–8).

The advocates of the teleological argument, however, carefully avoid comparing the universe to a vegetable, as doing so undermines the argument. As John H. Hick explains:

The universe is not particularly like a vast machine. One could equally plausibly liken it to a great inert animal such as a crustacean, or to a vegetable. In this case the design argument fails, for whether crustaceans and vegetables are or are not consciously designed is precisely the question at issue. (*Philosophy of Religion*, p. 25)

Perhaps the biggest difference between the universe and a machine is that a machine has an identifiable *purpose* whereas the universe does not. The fact that the universe functions in strict accordance with the laws of gravity, for example, does not mean that it is a giant machine functioning for some purpose. As Nietzsche says: 'Let us likewise beware of believing the universe is a machine; it is certainly not constructed so as to perform some operation, we do it far too great honour with the word "machine"' (*The Gay Science*, 109, in *A Nietzsche Reader*, p. 200).

Admittedly, certain parts of the universe have their own purposes. Living organisms perform functions and have purposes such as reproducing and obtaining food. But there are no grounds for supposing that just because a few, small, highly evolved parts of the universe work towards their own particular ends and goals that the universe as a whole must have an ultimate purpose. To conclude that the universe as a whole has an ultimate purpose because parts of it have their own purposes, is very much like concluding that there is an ultimate purpose to the existence of the human race simply because individual human beings make schemes and plans.

A purpose to the universe as a whole cannot be discovered through an examination of various parts of the universe, and neither is a purpose to the universe apparent when the universe is considered as a whole: galaxies, clusters of galaxies, countless stars living and dying. The universe is certainly awesome, but it is impossible to see from a perspective internal to the universe that it is, or could be, *for* something.

If the universe has a purpose then that purpose must be for something that transcends the universe. We would have to know the mind of God to know whether or not the universe has a purpose and what, if it has a purpose, that purpose is. But, of course, it is precisely the existence of God that is in question here. In seeking to argue teleologically from the nature of the universe to the existence of God, we cannot make assumptions about the nature of the universe based on the assumption that there is a God and then use those assumptions about the nature of the universe to 'prove' God exists.

Another of Hume's main criticisms of the teleological argument is that the universe is bound to *appear* designed because for it to exist at all it must have some degree of order and coherence, an intrinsic integration of its parts. The advocates of the teleological argument see the order and coherence of this universe as a special and peculiar feature, as though they were comparing it to other universes totally lacking order and coherence. However, not only do we not know of other universes, a degree of order and coherence must be intrinsic to any universe that can or does exist.

The universe appears all the more designed when we choose to view it as all conveniently arranged for our benefit; when we chose to ignore both the huge role that chance has played in our coming to be and the fact that the universe is not in any way adapted to us, but rather us to the universe. It is only because we are so well adapted to the universe from which we arose, that we are able, in a limited and temporary way, to adapt certain features of our environment to our own ends using our ingenuity. In doing so, however, we must always work with the universe, as the universe is not predisposed or designed to work with us or for us. Any apparent indications to the contrary are merely fortunate accidents or the result of good planning on *our* part. It is never *kindness* on the part of wind and wave that leads to a successful voyage, simply lucky chance and the captain's skill at anticipating likely weather conditions.

There is a tendency to view luck as providential, as a kindly force that consciously and deliberately works to assist us, but really luck is only ever pure, blind chance that happens to work in our favour. A person who declares, for instance, that it is a sign of intelligent design that the Earth is in the Goldilocks zone, just the right distance from the sun for life to thrive, forgets that there are millions of planets in the universe that are not the right distance from their star for life to occur.

Given that there are billions of planets in the universe, it stands to the laws of probability that there will be at least a few that are just the right size and distance from just the right kind of star for the basic conditions of life to be set. Eye-wateringly tiny though the probability may be – winning the National Lottery is a safe bet by comparison – we just happen to live on such a lucky planet. If we did not happen to live on such a planet then, of course, we would not exist to marvel at our remarkably rare and fortunate location in the cosmos and be tempted to attribute it to benign intention rather than blind chance.

With specific regard to life itself, the existence of life on Earth, and anywhere else for that matter, presupposes order-liness and adaptation to an environment, for life that was utterly disorderly and un-adapted to its environment could not live, could not have come about in the first place. When we watch Attenborough in HD and marvel at how well adapted living things are to their environment and to each other, it is as if we were comparing them to less marvellous living things that are not at all adapted, as though there could be such un-adapted creatures.

A person might still ask, however, what gives living things their orderliness and coherence, what gives them such a wonderful organization of parts? Hume's position is that nothing *gives* order, coherence and organization, they are simply intrinsic features of the universe, or at least features that are bound to emerge over time.

He offers the Epicurean hypothesis, arguing that a finite number of randomly moving particles will go through every possible combination in an unlimited amount of time. Eventually, a stable order with a self-perpetuating coherence and an ever-increasing complexity is bound to be arrived at. In some respects, this very basic hypothesis presages Darwin's theory of evolution, which identifies and describes a simple and utterly blind process by which random occurrences, random mutations, result in all the highly evolved, highly complex, apparently designed life forms that inhabit planet Earth, including ourselves.

Evolution – an unassailable theory

Hume had been dead seventy-five years when the theory of evolution exploded onto the world stage in the form of Darwin's *On the Origin of Species by Means of Natural Selection*. Had Hume known of the theory of evolution he would have embraced it with open arms, not only because he loved anything that undermines metaphysics and superstition, but because the theory is a clear scientific demonstration of the soundness of certain philosophical principles put forward in his *Dialogues Concerning Natural Religion*. The book attacks, for instance, the assumption that order is 'inseparably attached to thought' (*Dialogues Concerning Natural Religion*, p. 89), arguing that there are other, unthinking ordering principles such as generation, vegetation, instinct and gravity, which, outside of human civilisation, entirely govern the universe:

> You need only look around you, replied *Philo*, to satisfy yourself with regard to this question. A tree bestows order and organization on that tree, which springs from it, without knowing the order: An animal, in the same manner, on its offspring: A bird, on its nest: And instances of this kind are even more frequent in the world, than those of order, which arise from reason and contrivance. To say that all this order in animals and vegetables proceeds ultimately from design is begging the question; nor can that great point be ascertained otherwise than by proving *a priori*, both that order is, from its nature, inseparably attached to thought, and that it can never, of itself, or from original unknown principles, belong to matter. (*Dialogues Concerning Natural Religion*, p. 89)

In denying that thought and intelligence are ordering principles at work in the physical universe as a whole, Hume would readily agree with Darwin that intelligence, as we know it, is the result of evolution, a product of nature and not its driving force. There may or may not be a higher, transcendental intelligence, but even if there is, the empirical evidence is that nature functions without its involvement. If you are not yet convinced that these bold claims are correct, then understanding what evolution is and how it works, understanding how it produces what the evolutionary biologist, Richard Dawkins, calls 'the illusion of design and planning' (*The Blind Watchmaker*, p. 21), may serve to convince you.

Why do giraffes have long necks? Put this question to people and most of them will give the common-sense answer that giraffes have long necks to reach high leaves. Now, if giraffes have long necks *for the purpose* of reaching high leaves, then they must have been intentionally designed that way, which raises the question: what or who had the intention and did the designing?

It is surely absurd to suggest that once upon a time there was a hungry giraffe ancestor with a short neck who decided he and his descendants would grow long necks in order to reach those juicy leaves at the top of the trees. How could a mere giraffe will its own neck, let alone the necks of its descendants, to become longer? It is at this point that the notion of a higher intelligence with plans and purposes and the power to realize them enters the picture. *Nature*, some say, made the giraffe's neck long so it could reach high leaves. To view nature as purposeful in this way is to envisage it as godlike, and so there is not a lot of difference between saying nature made the giraffe's neck long to enable it to reach high leaves and God made the giraffe's neck long to enable it to reach high leaves.

There is a sound principle in philosophy supposedly formulated by the medieval philosopher, William of Ockham, known as *Ockham's razor*. The principle states that in seeking to explain something one should not posit more concepts than are absolutely necessary for the explanation to succeed. In short, the simplest explanations are the best.

In perfect accordance with Ockham's razor, the theory of evolution by means of natural selection explains why giraffes have long necks without resorting to problematic notions of purposeful, otherworldly, metaphysical powers – powers that are not empirically demonstrable. Indeed, the theory of evolution by means of natural selection explains why giraffes have long necks without resorting to any notion of purpose or intention whatsoever. 'Natural selection,' says Dawkins, 'is the blind watchmaker, blind because it does not see ahead, does not plan consequences, has no purpose in view' (*The Blind Watchmaker*, p. 21). Dawkins' use of the term 'blind watchmaker' is, of course, a comment on Paley's divine watchmaker.

The fossil record indicates that giraffes are descended from a deer-like ancestor with a short neck. Occasionally, due to a random mutation or variation in its genes, an individual organism belonging to that ancient species would be born with a slightly longer neck. Having a longer neck gave that individual an advantage in the competition for a share of the limited amount of food available in its particular environment. It could eat from slightly higher up every tree in its environment where others of its kind could not reach. It survived and thrived on its full stomach and went on to reproduce. Perhaps, being better fed than its rivals, it lived longer than they did and so reproduced more times than they did. Quite simply, because long necks in that particular species, in its particular environment, repeatedly gave a survival advantage over millions of years, the long neck gene kept getting *naturally selected* for reproduction, until the species we call giraffe evolved.

Actually, in the interests of scientific accuracy, it must be noted that recent research has sought to revise this classic view of the giraffe's neck, held by most biologists since Darwin. The claim is that it was not so much the *feeding* advantage of having a longer neck that led to the long neck gene being naturally selected, as the *fighting* advantage of having a longer neck. The males of several species compete for females by butting heads. Giraffes compete for females by bashing necks. In 'Winning By A Neck: Sexual Selection In the Evolution of Giraffe' (*The American Naturalist*, November 1996), Robert Simmons and Lue Scheepers present the case that it was competition for mates rather than competition for food that pushed the evolution of the giraffe's long neck. Simmons and Scheepers found that male giraffes with the longest, largest necks tend to win mating contests and so pass on their genes.

Whichever it was, feeding or fighting, and perhaps it was both (it is interesting that giraffes also have long legs and tongues), the key point is that it was the blind process of natural selection that produced the world's tallest mammal, not intelligent design. The giraffe was not created by a divine giraffe maker, it evolved.

All living things evolved by process of natural selection from simpler, more primitive organisms. Even the extremely high order functions of consciousness and intelligence are products of brain evolution by process of natural selection, even if consciousness cannot be adequately described in purely neurobiological terms and must be described in a non-scientific, non-reductive language that makes reference to *mental states* (see any introduction to the *philosophy of mind* for a consideration of the relationship between consciousness and the brain).

The science of genetics reveals that all living things are related and evolved from common ancestors; from basic single cell organisms that lived billions of years ago. When some members of a species become geographically isolated from the rest in a significantly different environment, different random variations are naturally selected in the isolated group than are naturally selected in the main group, until the isolated group becomes so different as to constitute a new species. This phenomenon is called *speciation* and is responsible for the Earth's huge variety of plant and animal species.

There is a lot more to the theory of evolution than can be captured in my brief summary, which is meant only to show that there is no need to resort to the problematic metaphysics of creationism to explain the diversity, complexity and environmental adaptation of life on Earth. If you want to know more about evolution there are, of course, thousands of books on the subject. If you do not want to begin at the very beginning with Darwin's world-changing masterpiece, *On the Origin of Species*, Dawkin's *The Blind Watchmaker* is a good place to start as it is designed by its author to be accessible to the general reader.

The more one learns about evolution by natural selection the more the evidence stacks up. Evolution is a scientific fact supported by an ever-growing wealth of empirical data from biology, embryology, genetics, geology and the fossil record. Religious people who simply try to deny the existence of evolution make fools of themselves. Denying evolution is like denying the Earth is round, and it is frankly outrageous and absurd that religious fundamentalists who are prepared to believe in miracles, which by definition defy empirical possibility, are disposed to dismiss the theory of evolution as unfounded nonsense. 'It is just a theory' they say, wanting to reduce all theories to the same low standing, and belief or disbelief in any theory to a matter of personal prejudice.

In response, it can be said that there are theories and there are theories. On the one hand, there are theories backed by sound, integrated, critically assessed evidence, while on the other hand, there are dubious, incoherent notions lacking any real evidence that hardly deserve to be called theories at all. Certainly, the scientific theory of evolution has vastly more evidence supporting it than any of the so-called theories ranged against it.

Somewhat more sensible religious thinking has tried to accommodate the theory of evolution by arguing that evolution is a tool employed by God to develop human life. In one version of so-called *theistic evolution* or *evolutionary creation*, God continually guides the tool, while in another, he simply created the first basic life forms that then began to evolve without any further intervention on his part. There is, however, no credible empirical evidence for this view, and any attempt to support it must resort to the theistic arguments we are currently engaged in rejecting.

There is also the problem of why God would resort to the extremely longwinded process of evolution to create mankind when, being omnipotent, he could have done it all at once. Why go the long way round? Then again, being eternal, there is no such thing as a long time for God, so perhaps for him it was not the long way round, just the simplest and cleverest way of doing things. Scientists are, of course, trying to explain how life emerged from inorganic matter, from a primordial chemical soup, without appealing in any way to the idea of God.

In his 1996 address to the Pontifical Academy of Sciences, Pope John Paul II accepted that the theory of evolution is 'more than an hypothesis' (*Magisterium Is Concerned with Question of Evolution for It Involves Conception of Man*, para. 4, 22 October 1996), and the official position of the Catholic Church remains more or less that set out by Pope Pius XII in his famous 1950 encyclical, *Humani Generis*: the human body may derive from 'pre-existent and living matter' (*Humani Generis*, para. 36, 12 August 1950) but the human soul comes directly from God.

Hume hammers home the final nail

Central to Hume's critique of the teleological argument is his solidly empiricist principle that more cannot be known about a cause than is known through its effect. If a person can see only one half of a pair of scales, and he sees the balance fully raised, then he can be certain that the weight on the hidden side is heavier than the weight on the visible side. He cannot know, however, that the weight on the hidden side is infinitely heavy or, indeed, whether it is one thing or several things. 'But it is still allowed to doubt,' says Hume, 'whether that weight be an aggregate of several distinct bodies, or one uniform united mass' (*Dialogues Concerning Natural Religion*, p. 78). The same argument, and the same scales analogy, is also found in Hume's *Enquiries Concerning Human Understanding*, where he says:

> If the cause, assigned for any effect, be not sufficient to produce it, we must either reject that cause, or add to it such qualities as will give it a just proportion to the effect. But if we ascribe to it farther qualities, or affirm it capable of producing other effects, we can only indulge the licence of conjecture, and arbitrarily suppose the existence of qualities and energies, without reason or authority. The same rule holds, whether the cause assigned be brute unconscious matter, or a rational intelligent being. (*Enquiries Concerning Human Understanding*. p. 136)

The point Hume is making is that because from an effect we can only infer a cause sufficient to produce that effect, the teleological argument exceeds the bounds of reason in claiming to prove the existence of a single, unified, infinite, all powerful, wholly benevolent God. Even if we could validly infer divine design of the universe from an empirical study of the universe, from an empirical study of *the effect*, we would only be entitled to posit a designer *sufficiently* powerful to produce the universe, not the infinitely powerful God of the Judeo-Christian tradition.

We could certainly say that the designer was very powerful and highly creative, as anything that produced the universe would have to have an abundance of these qualities, but we could neither assert or deny that the designer was the most powerful being that exists or could possibly exist. There might or might not be an infinitely more powerful being than the one that supposedly created the universe, we simply cannot know and certainly the teleological argument cannot help us to know.

Even if we could make an inference from the universe to a designer, we would 'indulge the licence of conjecture' if we claimed that there was only one designer or that he was perfectly good. For all we know, the universe could have been created by an army of gods, some of them more talented than others, some of them good, some of them evil. The fact that the universe contains many unpleasant things might be taken to suggest that evil gods had a hand in the design. Although, in the end, we simply cannot know one way or the other, supposing evil had a hand in the design is certainly no more of an odd conjecture than the conjecture that the universe indicates the existence of a single, perfectly good creator.

Hume argues that, 'From the moment the attributes of the deity are supposed finite' such 'strange suppositions' can be made 'and a thousand more of the same kind' (*Dialogues Concerning Natural Religion*, p. 79). Indulging in his own suppositions to make the point that the teleological argument can lead to a whole host of equally unverifiable claims regarding the nature of the divine, Hume says:

This world, for aught he knows, is very faulty and imperfect, compared to a superior standard; and was only the first rude essay of some infant deity, who afterwards abandoned it, ashamed of his lame performance: It is the work only of some dependent, inferior deity; and is the object of derision to his superiors: It is the production of old age and dotage in some superannuated deity; and ever since his death, has run on at adventures, from the first impulse and active force which it received from him. (*Dialogues Concerning Natural Religion*, p. 79)

What all this shows, above all else, is that the teleological argument, which is supposed to *prove* the existence of a single, all powerful, benevolent God, in fact, at best, merely *suggests* any one of a whole host of possible deities, without providing any means of proving the existence of any one of them, or even the means of showing one of them to be more likely than another. The teleological argument simply cannot do the job for which religion and the religious have long employed it.

The fourth way – the argument from degree

A lot of what has been said in this chapter has revolved around Aquinas' arguments for the existence of God. Even the ontological argument was linked to Aquinas as an argument that is notable by its absence from his five ways. Those of you who have really been paying attention will be aware that although a lot has been said about Aquinas' first, second and third *cosmological* ways, and about his fifth *teleological* way, nothing has yet been said about his fourth way: the argument from degree or gradation.

Like Aquinas' other arguments for God's existence, the argument from degree is *a posteriori* in that it begins with observation and experience of the universe. When we look at the world we find that things possess different degrees of perfection. Some instruments are more accurate than others, some lines are straighter than others, some circles are closer to being perfectly round than others, some people are better looking than others, some actions are more noble or moral than others and so on. We judge any particular thing as being more or less a certain thing by the degree to which it approximates to that which is most that thing.

Aquinas takes the example of hotness, saying, 'things are hotter and hotter the closer they approach to what is hottest' (*Summa Theologiae*, p. 26). That which is hottest is 'truest and best' (*Summa Theologiae*, p. 26) in the set of hot things. In any set of things there is always that which is truest and best, that which is most perfectly that kind of thing, that which most fully possesses whatever property is common to the whole set.

Following Aristotle, Aquinas argues that whatever is truest and best is most real, 'most fully in being' (*Summa Theologiae*, p. 26).

Importantly, for Aquinas, whatever is most real and fully in being, in terms of most fully possessing a particular property, is that which causes that property in other things. 'When many things possess some property in common, the one most fully possessing it causes it in the others' (*Summa Theologiae*, p. 26). Continuing with the example of heat, Aquinas argues that 'fire, the hottest of all things, causes all other things to be hot' (*Summa Theologiae*, p. 26). So, for there to be things that possess degrees of being, goodness, nobility, virtue and other perfections, there must be that which most fully possesses these perfections, that which causes degrees of perfection in things. That which most fully possesses these perfections, that which is most fully perfect, is called God.

In some respects the argument from degree echoes Plato's theory of forms, which we mentioned earlier during our consideration of the cosmological argument. In *The Republic* and elsewhere, Plato argues that the constantly changing, imperfect material world we see around us does not really exist. It is just a mere appearance or shadow cast by a higher reality that we cannot sense but can reason about. This higher reality is not physical but is comprised of perfect, unchanging, timeless, universal *forms* or ideas.

All the particular, imperfect circles in the world, for example, only exist as circles and are recognized as circles because they approximate towards the form of perfect circularity. Perfect circularity is truly real, whereas particular circles are merely imperfect shadows cast by perfect circularity. The forms are the source or cause of all reality and knowledge and there are forms corresponding to every type of particular thing in the world. The forms are arranged in a hierarchy, with the forms of qualities and concepts higher in the pyramid than the forms of physical things. At the top of the pyramid is the form of the Good, the supreme source or cause of everything including the forms.

It is hardly surprising that the argument from degree echoes to some extent Plato's theory of forms. The argument from degree is, after all, essentially Aristotelian, and Plato was Aristotle's teacher and major influence. Aristotle, however, was not a Platonist and Aquinas certainly was not, and to view the argument from degree as essentially Platonic produces more confusion than clarification. To explore the similarities and differences between the philosophies of Plato and Aristotle, two of the giants of Western philosophy, let alone take the perspective of Aquinas into account, no minnow himself, would require another book besides this one.

It must suffice to say, therefore, that perhaps the main difference between Aquinas' position and Plato's is that Aquinas does not see God as a Platonic form. Aquinas' idea of God is not Plato's idea of the Good. There are, of course, similarities. Both are the supreme being and ultimate source of all reality, but

Plato's Good is not envisaged as having the personal qualities that Aquinas' God is envisaged as having.

You may have become sufficiently sceptical by now about the techniques of medieval metaphysics – the sleight of hand by which God is conjured up at the end of an argument like a rabbit pulled from a hat – that you can already see what some of the problems with the fourth way are. Why not take a break and, using what you have learnt so far, try to think of as many criticisms of the fourth way as you can before you read on. After all, that is really *doing* philosophy, more so than reading this book, though the value of reading generally cannot be overestimated. It is certainly rewarding, and a good test of your growing philosophical knowledge and skills, to work out objections to an argument using your own powers of reason before you read up on those objections to confirm how right you were…

Why the argument from degree fails

In criticizing the fourth way, the argument from degree, we can immediately evoke Hume's empiricist principle, considered earlier, that more cannot be known about a cause than is know through the effect. The argument admits that things in the world are only more or less perfect. None of them is absolutely perfect because only God, a being that transcends the world, can be absolutely perfect. Hume's principle dictates, therefore, that whatever caused things in the world to be more or less perfect, if indeed anything did, only has to be more or less perfect itself and not absolutely perfect. And certainly from observing more or less perfect things in the world, from observing the effect, we cannot know that what caused them is absolutely perfect.

There may be many maximally perfect things, one for each type or genus of thing, rather than one maximally perfect thing. Each would be perfect in its own way. A possible reply to this might be that even if there are many maximally perfect things, each with its own kind of perfection, they all have perfection in common, a perfection that must ultimately come from that which is pure perfection, namely God. The real issue here, however, is that we cannot know whether or not there are many maximally perfect things. The fourth way states that things in the universe are only more or less perfect. Any maximally perfect things that might exist, therefore, would have to exist outside the universe, in which case we cannot know that they exist anymore than we can know that one absolutely perfect being exists. Why? Because, to repeat, we cannot know more about a cause than is known through the effect.

On a slightly different tack, it can be argued that in many categories of things perfection is not possible and is therefore a nonsensical notion. Perhaps there can be a perfect square or a perfect musical note, but how can there be perfect heat?

Arguably, perfect heat would have to be infinitely hot, otherwise a hotter and therefore more perfect heat would be possible. But surely, it is no more possible for something to be infinitely hot than it is possible for there to be an infinitely high number. Similarly, to talk about the perfect face or the perfect meal, except as a figure of speech, is nonsensical. There are clearly better and worse meals according to the quality of the ingredients and the skill of the chef, but there is no such thing as a perfect meal because how good a meal is has to be at least partly determined by the taste and appetite of the person eating it. One man's meat is another man's poison.

The fourth way argues that there must be a most perfect thing of any type in order for there to be things that are more or less perfect. This is simply incorrect. There does not have to be an absolute best, or even an absolute worst, for there to be, and for us to recognize, *better than* and *worse than*. In maths, for example, *greater than* (>) and *less than* (<) are understood without any notion of a greatest possible number. Indeed, we know there is no greatest possible number because the series of numbers is infinite.

We do not need an idea of the most perfect thing of any type in order to identify things of that type as more or less perfect. To judge David Beckham to be a better footballer than UK prime minister David Cameron there does not have to be a perfect footballer against which we compare the two Davids' different levels of footballing ability. We simply need to compare each to the other by watching them play and decide who is best at achieving the objectives peculiar to football.

For Aquinas, that which is 'most fully in being' (*Summa Theologiae*, p. 26) is God. But what is most fully in being might not be God. It might simply be energy, which can never be created or destroyed, or atoms, which remain fully in being while the things that are formed from them come into and go out of being. Such ideas were explored earlier during our consideration of the cosmological argument.

Finally, the fourth way leans heavily on the outdated Aristotelian science that we criticized earlier when examining the contingency and necessity argument. To repeat what was said then, it is simply not the case that actual x must be caused by that which is already actual x. Aquinas is right that fire is the hottest of all things, if we take fire to include the thermonuclear reactions taking place in the hottest stars, but it does not follow, as he argues, that it is fire that causes all other things to be hot. Heat is not always caused by that which is hot. Significant heat is generated, for example, when sodium and water, both at room temperature, are brought together to produce an exothermic reaction.

The moral argument

There is a link between the fourth way and the so-called *moral argument*, the final argument we will consider for God's existence. This is because the fourth way argues from degrees of perfection and goodness, including degrees of moral value, to absolute perfection, goodness and moral value.

Many philosophers who reject the ontological, cosmological and teleological arguments for God's existence on the grounds stated, are nonetheless convinced by the moral argument. That the world, or at least the human world, contains a moral dimension, that humans have a moral conscience, that we are capable of moral judgement, that there are moral facts and standards, is for them clinching proof of God's existence. All this, they argue, can only be made possible by the existence of a supremely moral being.

They reason that moral conscience, for example, the sense of right and wrong that governs most people's thoughts and actions, that causes them to suffer guilt and anxiety or to enjoy peace of mind, can only have been bestowed upon them by a being that is the very essence of moral goodness. Conscience, indeed, is still seen by many to be the voice of God within us, an inner angel telling us what we *ought* to do, and in the past virtually everyone saw conscience this way.

In the modern world we tend to draw a distinction between the moral and the religious, but in earlier cultures there was really no such distinction. Moral duty was indistinguishable from religious duty. To act morally was to do God's will, to act immorally was to defy him.

In 'Morality and Religion' H. O. Mounce takes the example of the ancient Hebrew attitude to the Ten Commandments. Nowadays, we tend to view the first four commandments as setting out religious duties to God, and the remaining six as setting out moral duties to neighbours. The ancient Hebrews, however, made no such distinction and saw all ten commandments as concerned with duties to God. As Mounce says, 'Thus the last six do not instruct us in how to serve our neighbour as distinct from serving God. Rather they instruct us in how God wishes us to serve him in our dealings with our neighbour' ('Morality and Religion', in *Philosophy of Religion: A Guide to the Subject*, p. 253).

The story of Moses receiving the Ten Commandments from God on tablets of stone (Exodus 20) illustrates in a graphic and unsophisticated way, that any fool can understand, the perceived unity of morality and divine will. For people who take the Bible literally, which in the past was just about everyone, there can be no clearer illustration that it is God's will that gives meaning to moral concepts such as duty and justice.

As to the *force* of moral imperatives, that was seen, and is still seen by many, to derive from the promise of rewards and the threat of punishments to be dealt out by God in an afterlife. Without God, so the argument goes, moral rules would lack authority, there would be no ultimate sanction against doing evil, no reason to do good. Indeed, without God, no distinction between good and bad behaviour could be made. Life would be a free-for-all where anything goes. In summary, morality has long been seen to imply God because morality is *of* God, a direct expression of his will backed by his authority.

Kant, whose genius did so much to undermine arguments for the existence of God based on what he calls 'speculative reason', formulates his own moral argument for the existence of God in his *Critique of Practical Reason*, where he claims that the immortality of the soul and the existence of God are both postulates of pure practical reason (*Critique of Practical Reason*, pp. 102–14). Kant sees what many less sophisticated advocates of the moral argument have failed to see: that moral truths must be independent of God otherwise they are nothing but the arbitrary whims of God. If morality depended entirely on God's will, then 'God is good' would be a mere truism as God would remain good whatever he willed.

This point was considered in Chapter 1, not with reference to Kant, but with reference to Plato's Euthyphro dilemma. Kant argues that it is not the case that 'X is good because God wills it', but rather that 'God wills x because it is good.' So, Kant's moral argument is not the claim that there must be a God because morality is God's will. Rather, his moral argument is that there must be a God, as only God can make it possible for people to achieve the perfect moral state of the *summum bonum* (highest good).

Kant argues that the highest good is achieved when a person becomes both completely virtuous and completely happy. This highest good is the objective of all moral action and a person is under a moral obligation to achieve it. This obligation is not dictated by the will of God but by a person's own reason. Kant equates moral action with rational action. To act morally is to act rationally in accordance with what Kant calls the *categorical imperative*. A person should only perform actions that can be universalized without contradiction, as acting in this way is rational. It is immoral and irrational to tell lies, for example, because telling lies is not a practice that can be universalized; it is not something that everyone could do all the time and it still remain possible for anyone to do it.

Now, a person can only be under the rational/moral obligation to achieve the highest good if it is possible to achieve it. Kant argues that *ought* implies *can*, that a person is only under a moral obligation to achieve x if it is logically possible to do so. Kant thought that it was logically possible for a person to achieve the highest good, but not necessarily in one lifetime. Practical difficulties mean that while a person can achieve virtue in this world, it is beyond their power to ensure that their virtue is rewarded with happiness.

A look at the world reveals that there are some virtuous people who are not happy, perhaps because they suffer pain and abuse, and there are certainly many other people who are happy but not virtuous. In order for it to be logically possible to achieve the highest good, to achieve the coincidence of virtue and happiness, in order for there to be a genuine moral obligation to *strive* to achieve it in this life, it must be possible to achieve it after death. God must be postulated, argues Kant, as the only being capable of facilitating the eventual harmonization of virtue and happiness that morality aims at and requires.

As the deepest of deep thinkers, Kant is not the easiest philosopher to grasp at the best of times, and certainly this argument is obscure even by his standards. Even to get the gist of it you may need to reread it several times. Rereading is not only normal but essential when it comes to studying all but the most basic philosophical passages. It might help to further familiarize yourself with the fundamentals of Kant's moral theory, which you will find outlined in any introduction to ethics.

The gist of what Kant is saying seems to be this: There is no guarantee of justice in this world. The virtuous are not necessarily rewarded with the happiness that ought to complement their virtue. Therefore, there must be the God-given guarantee of justice in the next world.

In a sense, Kant's position is comparable to that of Buddhism which recognizes that the highest good, the state of perfect blessedness or bliss known as *nirvana*, is not achievable in one lifetime. What the Buddhists claim must be achieved over many lifetimes, through many reincarnations, Kant claims must be achieved in the hereafter. Kant was a devout Christian, but his motive in formulating this argument was perhaps not so much to endorse a broadly Christian world-view, as to rescue human existence from a kind of *moral futility* in which it ultimately makes no difference whether one strives to live the life of Adolph Hitler or Mahatma Gandhi.

Why the moral argument fails

In order to reject the moral argument for God's existence it is necessary to show that there is no essential link between morality and God as the argument supposes. Philosophers have sought to do this partly by showing that the idea that morality is God-given leads to absurdities, and partly by showing that it is possible to make sense of what morality is and how it works in entirely secular terms without any appeal to divine will, decree, sanction or intervention.

Traditionally, moral conscience has been identified as the most obvious link between human beings and God, but it is highly doubtful that conscience is the God-given moral compass that it has long been characterized as. To begin with, some people clearly do not have a conscience. Psychopaths and socio-paths can commit atrocities without experiencing any sense of remorse. If conscience is God-given then surely God would have the power to make sure everyone had one. Admittedly, this is not the strongest argument against conscience because it can be countered that everyone has a conscience but that it is possible to ignore it, or that evil forces can so quieten the voice of a person's inner angel that it cannot be heard.

The real problem with conscience is its characterization as an *infallible* inner capacity for distinguishing right from wrong. There were Nazis who believed so sincerely in the rightness of the extermination programme that they saw carrying it out as a matter of conscience, and suffered pangs of guilt and anxiety if they failed to meet their quota of killings. If conscience was an infallible, inner, God-given capacity to distinguish right from wrong then it could not make such mistakes. We are able to identify those Nazis who acted on conscience as morally mistaken and confused because we are able to apply *objective* moral standards in judging them. If there were no objective moral standards, only the *subjective* standard of conscience, then we would be forced to the absurd conclusion that what the Nazis did was morally right because their consciences deemed it to be so.

All this strongly suggests that conscience itself cannot be the measure of what is right and wrong, that there is really no such thing as conscience as traditionally understood. The sense of right and wrong that many people undoubtedly have is not an innate, God-given capacity, but something that is acquired through experience, socialization and education. Its source is empirical not metaphysical. If people are generally disposed or even predisposed to behave morally, this is not because they have a God-given conscience, but because acting morally, acting with some degree of consideration for others, more often than not serves their physical and emotional needs as evolved social animals.

Just as goodness cannot be whatever conscience says it is, so goodness cannot be whatever God says it is. This point brings us back once again to the Euthyphro dilemma, the Euthyphro question. As we saw above, the only sensible answer to the Euthyphro question is the one that Kant gives: 'God wills x because it is good.' The alternative: 'X is good because God wills it' leads to the absurd conclusion that goodness is rooted in nothing but the arbitrary whims of God, and that doing good is, as J. L. Mackie says, 'merely prudent but slavish conformity to the arbitrary demands of a capricious tyrant' (*Ethics: Inventing Right and Wrong*, p. 230).

Now, to conclude that 'God wills x because it is good' has the important consequence of revealing moral principles and values to be as independent of God as mathematical principles and values. Morality is revealed as autonomous, as a phenomenon that can be studied without reference to God and religion, as a phenomenon that does not imply the existence of God.

Recognizing that morality is autonomous allows goodness to be identified with the best ways to live as a human social animal, rather than with the best ways to serve God. Removing God from the sphere of the ethical allows morality to be seen, not as a set of commandments delivered from on high, as something imposed on humankind from outside, but for what it really is, a functional device that has evolved along with human intelligence and civilization for ensuring many of the most basic and vital requirements of social life.

Although it may lend morality greater weight to give the impression that it is literally or metaphorically set in stone by God, that it is backed by the threat of divine punishment and the promise of divine reward, morality was *invented* in response to human needs. Its rules, or what might be more accurately described as its norms, habits, customs, attitudes, emotive prescriptions and so on, have evolved and been refined overtime, and are constantly modified according to changing circumstances. Its rules are objective, not in an abstract, absolute, context-independent way, but in the way that the rules of a game are very real in the context of that game: regulating and facilitating play, allowing the game to proceed, allowing there to be a game at all.

Morality is not rooted in the metaphysical, it is rooted in us. It is rooted in species-specific physical and emotional requirements, in natural human passions that are by turns selfish and altruistic, in the constantly pressing demand from reality to devise cooperative strategies for achieving, maintaining, protecting and enhancing what people need and generally want as highly sexed, highly active, highly intelligent, highly touchy social animals.

The best example of a wholly secular moral theory is probably utilitarianism. Overtly empiricist, it seeks to distinguish between right and wrong entirely on the basis of an empirical analysis of the *utility* of human actions, deliberately avoiding any appeal to religious, metaphysical or abstract reasoning in formulating its principles. The nineteenth-century English philosopher, John Stuart Mill, the major exponent of utilitarianism, says, 'It is proper to state that I forgo any advantage which could be derived to my argument from the idea of abstract right, as a thing independent of utility' (*On Liberty*, p. 15). For utilitarianism, there are no absolute moral values as such. Actions cannot be judged as intrinsically moral or immoral. All actions must be morally evaluated, and can only be morally evaluated, according to their utility in particular circumstances. Actions are of utility – useful and helpful – to the extent that they promote happiness. As Mill says:

> The creed which accepts as the foundation of morals, Utility or the Greatest Happiness Principle, holds that actions are

right in proportion as they tend to promote happiness, wrong as they tend to produce the reverse of happiness. By happiness is intended pleasure and the absence of pain; by unhappiness, pain and the privation of pleasure. (*Utilitarianism*, p. 137)

There is a lot more to utilitarianism than this, but there is no need to say more about it now as the aim here is not to provide a detailed account of utilitarianism, but simply to show, by means of a concrete example, that secular morality is not only possible but actual. The actuality of secular morality could have been shown just as well by outlining Aristotle's virtue theory, which provides down to earth, practical guidance on how best to flourish as a human being and achieve the earthly state of profound happiness and contentment that the ancient Greeks called *eudaimonia*. Virtue for Aristotle lies in having a balanced character attuned to the world and other people rather than in obedience to the dictates of religion.

By way of conclusion to this chapter I shall return to Kant's distinctive moral argument and offer a few criticisms of it. On a general note, it can be argued that Kant's conception of morality is far too grandiose. Do people really aim to achieve the ideal of the *summum bonum*, the highest good that is the complete harmonization of virtue and happiness, or is morality in fact a far more mundane and pragmatic affair?

An empirical assessment of people's moral conduct appears to reveal that they aim only at having a decent, bearable life alongside others: at enjoying the love, respect and support of others and so on. Kant perhaps elevates morality too high: needlessly, metaphysically high, using it to rebuild the bridge to God he so brilliantly demolishes elsewhere in his writings. Interestingly, Kantian ethics is normally taught from an entirely secular perspective that makes no mention of his God postulate. Kant's moral theory seems more tenable when the God postulate is set aside and the focus is placed entirely on our rational duty to treat other people as ends in themselves rather than as mere means to an end.

Kant was a devout Christian, so perhaps he felt he needed to offer a clever argument of his own for God's existence having trashed all the rest. In Nietzsche's view, Kant's moral theory is inspired by his religious prejudices. Indeed, it reeks of piety:

> The tartuffery [hypocritical piety], as stiff as it is virtuous, of old Kant as he lures us along the dialectical bypaths which lead, more correctly, mislead, to his 'categorical imperative' – this spectacle makes us smile, we who are fastidious and find no little amusement in observing the subtle tricks of old moralists and moral-preachers. (*Beyond Good and Evil*, p. 36)

Although there may be some truth in what Nietzsche says about Kant, and his words support my suggestion that Kant elevates morality needlessly high, we are both guilty here of a practice that is generally frowned upon in philosophy: *argumentum ad hominem* (argument against the man). Nietzsche, in fact, is just about the only philosopher who is allowed to get away with it. He is even admired for doing it. Perhaps because he does it so well, with exquisite, measured nastiness. *Argumentum ad hominen* is generally outlawed in philosophy because philosophy proceeds by criticizing a philosopher's arguments, not his or her motives for making them. Just as in soccer one should play the ball not the man, in philosophy one should play the argument not the man.

A standard objection to Kant's moral argument itself, one that is reminiscent of the kind of criticisms that Hume makes in his *Dialogues Concerning Natural Religion*, is this: It is an assumption on Kant's part that only God can bring about the *summum bonum*. It could just as well be brought about by a host of demi-gods, none of which is a supreme being. As Brian Davies puts it:

> Why cannot the highest good be successfully promoted by something other than people but different from what God is supposed to be? Why cannot a top-ranking angel do the job? Why not a pantheon of angels? Why not a pantheon of angels devoted to the philosophy of Kant? (*An Introduction to the Philosophy of Religion*, p. 270)

So, Kant's moral argument, like all the other arguments we have considered for the existence of a supreme, all powerful, intelligent, morally perfect being, fails to *prove* the existence of such a being.

4

Evil and God

Some people believe in the existence of the Devil, a personal, wholly evil being who is the enemy of God. If the Devil exists then he presents us with a philosophical problem, quite apart from all the other trouble he causes in the world. The problem is a well-known one that has probably crossed your mind many times before. If God is all powerful and perfectly good then why does he tolerate the existence of the Devil? If God is omnipresent then how can the Devil have his domain? The Bible tells us that the Devil is of God, a fallen angel, but how can that which is of God be less than perfectly good?

We are not going to investigate whether or not the Devil exists as such. Rather, we will focus on the theological problem raised by the undeniable existence of what the Devil stands for: all the evil and suffering in the world. If there is an all powerful, benevolent God then why does he tolerate evil and suffering in the world? Surely he has the *power* to end evil and suffering but he does not. Surely he must *want* to end evil and suffering but he does not. These points capture the essence of what has come to be known in the philosophy of religion as the *problem of evil*.

Some people respond to the problem of evil by concluding that the existence of evil and suffering in the world clearly shows that there simply cannot be an all powerful, benevolent God. If there was such a God, evil and suffering would not be tolerated. Over the centuries the problem of evil has caused many people to lose their faith in God. People who have witnessed an innocent child die painfully of disease or the bloody massacre of their entire family by terrorists have concluded that God does not exist because God would not allow such things to happen. For some, the single most powerful argument against the existence of God can be captured in one word: Auschwitz. As many have asked since, 'Where was God at Auschwitz?'

Other people, who insist for whatever reason on continuing to believe in God, have sought to overcome the problem of evil by seeking to *reconcile* the existence of an all powerful, benevolent being with the blatant existence of evil and suffering. Any such attempt at reconciliation is known as *theodicy*: a justification of the ways of God to man. Much of this chapter will involve an exploration of theodicy, an exploration of the various *theodicies* that have been put forward by philosophers and theologians over the centuries. Before exploring these theodicies, however, we need to set out the problem of evil in more precise terms than we have so far. To begin with, we need to familiarize ourselves with an important distinction that has long been made between two different types of evil.

Natural evil and moral evil

Those pondering the problem of evil have long divided the many troubles of mankind into *natural evil* on the one hand and *moral evil* on the other.

Natural evil includes all the suffering caused by natural phenomena that people are not responsible for: volcanoes, earthquakes, tsunamis, meteorite strikes, disease, old age and natural death. What Shakespeare describes as 'The heart-ache and the thousand natural shocks that flesh is heir to' (*Hamlet*, Act 3, Scene 1).

Moral evil includes all the suffering caused by human actions that people are responsible for. Every evil that flows from the seven deadly sins of wrath, greed, sloth, pride, lust, envy and gluttony: theft, fraud, abuse, rape, torture, assault and murder – all the nasty, spiteful, selfish things people do to each other on a daily basis. What the poet Robert Burns describes as 'Man's inhumanity to man' ('Man was made to Mourn').

The distinction between natural and moral evil makes good sense and we can all relate to it. It is a useful distinction to have in mind when it comes to exploring the various theodicies. Like most distinctions, however, it is not entirely clear cut. Natural evil, so-called natural disasters, can often be caused by moral evil, or at least be exacerbated by it. A particular famine, for example, may appear to be an entirely natural disaster rooted in drought, pestilence and crop failure, but a closer look reveals that war, corruption and poorly maintained transport infra-structure are largely to blame.

The Japanese tsunami of 2011 was clearly a natural disaster, an example of natural evil, as mankind cannot cause or control earthquakes. The ongoing tragedy of the Fukushima Daiichi nuclear power plant that began with the tsunami, however, is not simply part and parcel of that natural disaster. The reactors at the plant exploded as a result of moral evil in the form of negligence and lack of foresight. Had the plant been built to withstand the large tsunami that actually hit it, rather than the small tsunami those wishing to cut costs predicted would hit it, had there been sufficient backup systems in place to continue running the water pumps that cooled the reactors, then the reactors would not have overheated and exploded.

As said, the distinction between natural and moral evil is useful, but every case of evil and suffering has to be judged on its own merits in order to decide whether it is a case of natural or moral evil. Often it is a mixture of both. In some cases it is very difficult if not impossible to judge how much of the blame lies with people and how much lies with natural circumstances.

Spelling out the problem of evil

The problem of evil does not arise as such for those who do not insist that there is an all powerful, benevolent God. It is a specifically theological problem for theists who insist for whatever reason that there is a God. Theists face the problem or dilemma of evil precisely because they insist that the following three seemingly incompatible propositions are all true:

1 God is omnipotent.

2 God is all-good.

3 There is evil and suffering in the world.

Set out like this the problem can be seen as a logical one. It appears to be logically impossible that all three of these propositions can be true together. Now, propositions 1 and 2 are held to be true as a matter of faith, Scripture, belief in the validity of the theistic arguments or religious indoctrination. For theists, the truth of propositions 1 and 2 is non-negotiable. Proposition 3 is known to be true as a matter of empirical observation. Who but a fool or a very innocent child would deny that the world is full of evil and suffering? To spell out the incompatibility of the three propositions:

If 1 and 3 are true then 2 cannot be true. An omnipotent God has the power to prevent evil. That such a God does not prevent evil must be because he is not all-good and therefore does not want to. If 2 and 3 are true then 1 cannot be true. An all-good God would want to prevent evil. That such a God does not prevent evil must be because he lacks the power to do so.

Both these alternatives are entirely unacceptable to theists for whom, as said, the existence of an omnipotent, all-good God is non-negotiable. For theists, a means absolutely has to be found whereby all three propositions can be held to be true together. Proposition 3 has to be made compatible with 1 and 2 without in any way weakening 1 and 2. Proposition 3 has to be *justified* in light of 1 and 2. Any such justification, or attempt at such justification, is called theodicy.

Theodicy – the free will defence

One theodicy that still remains highly influential in theology is that of the late Roman, early Christian scholar, Augustine of Hippo, better known as Saint Augustine. Born in North Africa in 354, Augustine converted to Christianity in his thirties and spent his life developing Christian thought in light of classical Greek and Roman philosophy. He was particularly interested in the Neoplatonism of Plotinus and is certainly significantly responsible for the vein of broadly Platonic ideas that runs through Christianity. If, as Nietzsche says, 'Christianity is Platonism for "the people"' (*Beyond Good and Evil*, p. 32), then Augustine certainly played a role in making it so.

Present-day Christians are fond of saying that evil is the absence of God, a claim that reflects ideas found in the writings of Augustine. Augustine argues that evil is not a substance, something that God created, but rather a privation or lack in a substance. Illness, for example, is not something that exists in its own right, but is rather a lack of good health. In claiming that evil is not one of God's creations, but rather something that can happen to one of God's creations, this argument seeks to fundamentally separate God from evil and show how both can 'be' at the same time. It avoids insisting on the impossibility of their co-existence by arguing that God exists in a wholly positive way, whereas evil 'exists' only in a wholly negative way as a privation or lack of existence.

The question remains, however, as to why God, being omnipotent, did not make the whole of creation corruption-proof? Augustine's answer to this is that God created the universe *ex nihilo* rather than *ex Deo* – out of nothing rather than out of God. Had God created the universe out of himself it would not be genuinely distinct from him. As part of him it would remain perfect, but it would also lack any real objectivity or autonomy. In creating the universe *ex nihilo*, God created a genuinely independent universe. A universe created by a perfect being according to an ideal of perfection, but a universe in which any particular being can become less than perfect, can become corrupted and deprived by ceasing to be all that God meant it to be.

With particular regard to the highest sentient beings, which for Augustine includes the angels and mankind, this corruption is the result of free will. Responding to questions raised at the beginning of this chapter regarding the Devil, Augustine would answer that although the Devil was created by a perfect God, he was created with free will and hence with the capacity to choose to turn against God. Interestingly, the claim is that angels and men are far greater creations for having free will, far greater expressions of God's creative genius, than they would be if they were mere puppets incapable of acting against God's will.

The notion of free will is central to the Augustinian theodicy and all the Augustinian-type theodicies that it has inspired, and certainly the so-called *free will defence* is by far the most frequently offered solution to the problem of evil. As Augustine recognizes, The Bible itself explains or justifies the existence of evil in the world in terms of human free will.

In the beginning, everything was perfect in the Garden of Eden. The Fall, the casting out of Adam and Eve from the

Garden of Eden into a world of pain and suffering (Genesis 3.15–19), came about because of Adam and Eve's original sin, their free choice to give way to temptation and do what God had forbidden them to do, which was to eat fruit from the tree of knowledge. The Eden myth seeks to make it clear that all the evil that plagues mankind, both natural and moral, was caused by human choice, not God.

It is interesting to ask, as something of an aside, if Adam and Eve could really have been morally responsible for eating the fruit, if it was eating the fruit that gave them knowledge of good and bad? Before eating the fruit they were naïve and innocent, so surely they could not have known that what they were doing was wrong. One possible reply is that they did not know eating the fruit was wrong, but they did know that God had forbidden it. But if they were innocent then they had no understanding that it was wrong to disobey God. It has also been asked why God created the tree of knowledge in the first place and why he put it in the middle of the garden of Eden as an obvious temptation? In picking over the details of the Eden myth, one begins to suspect that Adam and Eve were set up, but we shall let that pass on the grounds that tangling with the details of Scripture as though it were literally true is a fool's errand unbecoming of serious philosophers.

It is highly unlikely, to say the least, that the Eden myth is literally true. The world is far older than the Eden story supposes and science shows that we are not descended from Adam and Eve. It is also surely absurd to suggest that there is evil in the world simply because we are all still being punished because Adam and Eve scrumped God's special fruit thousands of years ago. But of course, it does not matter that the Eden myth is not literally true. Today, only very unsophisticated or very brain-washed people believe that the Eden myth is literally true and that it is important that it be literally true. What matters, as with all myths, legends and fables, is what the Eden myth symbolizes and the point that it makes.

The point the Eden myth makes is that moral evil at least, what religion calls *sin*, results entirely from human freedom and choice. If we give way to the temptation to do evil, as a fictional Eve gave way to being tempted by the Devil in the guise of a serpent, it is because we choose to give way. We are to blame, we alone are responsible. If God were to intervene to stop us from sinning, which if he exists as defined he surely has the power to do, he could do so only by taking away our free will and reducing us to perfectly behaved automata. He could do so only by making us far less than we are, only by removing the free will that is the essence of what we are.

Not least, as automata, we could not come to love God as, so it is said, he wants us to. Only a free being can truly love because love that cannot not be given is not true love. Love must be a choice to love. Arguably, God had to create creatures with the capacity to turn away from him in order that they might grow to genuinely love him.

One of the main objections to the free will defence is that it is not logically impossible for there to be genuinely free beings who always choose good. That a person always chooses the same kind of thing does not mean that they are not free. Their freedom does not consist in sometimes choosing the opposite kind of thing, but in the fact that they *could* have chosen the opposite kind of thing even though they chose not to. In order to be free, a person does not have to sometimes choose good and sometimes choose evil, he could be free and always choose good, just as he could be free and always choose evil. God, arguably, could have created people who always choose good, but he did not. That he did not is inconsistent with the claim that he is all-good and all powerful. As J. L. Mackie puts it:

> If there is no logical impossibility in a man's freely choosing the good on one, or on several occasions, there cannot be a logical impossibility in his freely choosing the good on every occasion. God was not, then, faced with a choice between making innocent automata and making beings who, in acting freely, would sometimes go wrong: there was open to him the obviously better possibility of making beings who would act freely but always go right. Clearly, his failure to avail himself of this possibility is inconsistent with his being both

omnipotent and wholly good. ('Evil and Omnipotence', in *Mind*, 1955, p. 209)

Augustine argues that God always foresaw the fall into evil of both angels and mankind. It was because he foresaw this fall that he was able to plan mankind's redemption through the coming of Christ. Arguably, if God foresaw that mankind would fall into evil then he is ultimately responsible for that evil because he went ahead and created mankind despite what he knew. Against this, it can be argued that people are still responsible for their own actions despite God's foresight regarding their actions.

Even if there is some sense in saying that God acted somewhat irresponsibly in creating creatures capable of evil, the real issue seems to be whether or not the project is on balance worthwhile despite the fact that people do bad things. One can only speculate that if God exists and he created mankind, he must have thought that the project of creating mankind was on balance worthwhile, the good ultimately outweighing the evil, the love outweighing the hate, otherwise he would not have embarked on it.

Theodicy – soul making

Questionable though it is, the free will defence offers some justification of moral evil, but it offers little or no justification of natural evil. For an attempt to justify natural evil we must look to the philosopher Irenaeus and what has come to be known as the *Irenaean theodicy*.

Saint Irenaeus was one of the very earliest Christian scholars. A Greek born in what is now Turkey in the first half of the second century, he became Bishop of Lyon. He helped to establish the authority of the Church of Rome, not least by attacking in his writings various early Christian sects and accusing them of heresy: deviation from the true message of Christ according to the Gospels. It was in his major work, *Against Heresies*, that he established the notion that natural evil is vital to the process of soul-making.

One early Christian sect that Irenaeus accused of heresy was the Gnostics. The Gnostics held the heretical belief – heretical according to Irenaeus – that the world was not created by God but by a subordinate, less than perfect demiurge. This was a common view in certain pre-Christian, pagan religions that, alongside the teachings of Christ, significantly influenced Christian Gnosticism. For the Gnostics, the view that the world was created by a less than perfect demiurge explained why there is imperfection and natural evil.

In insisting, against the Gnostics, that the world was created directly by God, who is wholly perfect, Irenaeus has to explain and justify the existence of imperfection and natural evil in some other way. His extremely anthropocentric justification of natural evil is that it exists to enable the human soul to mature through suffering and adversity. Summarizing Irenaeus' view, Peter Cole says, 'The presence of evil helps people to grow and develop' (*Philosophy of Religion*, p. 70). Natural evil, therefore, is actually a good thing, or at least a necessary thing, because without it the human soul cannot be perfected.

Irenaeus holds that the only real difference between humans and animals at birth is that humans have a huge potential for moral and spiritual development. In order to reach their potential, in order to become rational and moral beings that resemble God and are capable of a relationship with God, humans must go through a long, hard process of soul-making. The Irenaean theodicy, like the Augustinian theodicy, emphasizes the importance of human free will. It is the exercise of free will in face of the endless difficulties and adversities of life that eventually forges the mature, wise, virtuous human soul. Irenaeus sees the world as a kind of assault course set up by God to build up human character and lick it into shape, a gymnasium for the spirit that exists for the purpose of turning out beings worthy of God's seal of approval.

The Irenaean theodicy justifies evil as a means to an end, and certainly in everyday life we view minor evils, though not major ones, as good to the extent to which they serve either to avoid a greater evil or bring about a good that could not otherwise have been achieved. In our dealings with children especially – selfish, reckless creatures in dire need of moral and spiritual shaping – we often recognize the value of 'tough love' and being 'cruel to be kind'.

For example, not knowing any better and being subject to appetite rather than reason, a child who is given the opportunity to do so will gorge on junk food. An adult must intervene to stop the child and change his diet before he begins to suffer from obesity and ill health. The child will see this intervention to stop him eating what he most desires as mean and evil, but the adult will know that it is a *necessary* evil perpetrated for the purpose of producing a greater good in the form of a slim, healthy body. By utilizing a series of minor evils – cancelling the cola, shelving the snacks, insisting on the salad – a greater good is brought about.

Certainly, minor evils, and even some quite significant evils, can produce a greater good. The world is full of examples of people who have been shaped for the better morally and spiritually by significant misfortune, including ill health and even disability. But what about extreme evil? The claim that evil exists for the purpose of producing a greater good, that it can be justified on that basis, seems to break down completely when we consider the very worst evils.

Surely, no consequences of the Holocaust, for example, can justify the evils of the Holocaust. No good that came of the Holocaust, such as developments in human rights law, can possibly diminish, dilute, offset, redefine, warrant, validate or excuse the pure evil that took place. It would be crass for anyone to claim, at any future point in human history, that the Holocaust or any other similar mass extermination – and there have been many – was 'worth it' because it led to this or that good.

As for the people who suffered and died in the Holocaust, the concentration camps did little or nothing for most of them in terms of soul-making. They were not made stronger, they were killed, and if they were not killed they were generally left weakened and traumatized for the rest of their lives. As Cole says, 'Indeed, in the Holocaust, people were ruined and destroyed more than made or perfected. It is hard to see how this fits God's design and human progress' (*Philosophy of Religion*, p. 71).

It can be asked, as a further criticism of the Irenaean theodicy, why God, being all powerful, does not create ready-made mature souls? If he can create such souls without the need for evil, which surely he can, then evil is not justified as a means to an end. In response, it can be argued that a soul that has matured to goodness as a result of its own free, autonomous activity, and come to love God of its own accord, is of more value than a soul possessing ready-made goodness. As said, God wants creatures who choose to love him, because only love that is freely given is genuine love. Creatures that were ready-made to love God, that could not do otherwise, would not be capable of genuine love.

One final objection to the Irenaean theodicy: natural evil is not justified because soul-making could be achieved simply by meeting pleasant challenges rather than by overcoming terrible adversities. Bad things are not the only occurrences in life that are character building. A person also develops by learning skills and achieving goals, so why is it not possible for the soul to be forged by these positive things alone? In response, it can be argued that climbing mountains, actual and metaphorical, in the certainty that nothing can go seriously wrong, would not be enough to develop true character, wisdom and virtue. A person can only develop spiritually by undergoing real physical and emotional extremes, by confronting real dangers and suffering real heartaches, by being in the world as it is and as it must surely be.

It seems Augustine, Irenaeus and other saintly philosophers make a reasonably good job of reconciling the existence of an omnipotent, wholly good God with the existence of evil and suffering in the world. There is moral evil because, for good reasons, humans are made free. There is natural evil because humans can only develop spiritually in a world that is *real*, a world that contains genuine adversities, misfortunes, heartaches and pains. It all sounds very plausible, *if* there is a God.

Perhaps Irenaeus could have offered a far simpler justification of natural evil: there is so-called natural evil simply because the world is real as opposed to artificial. In creating a full-on reality, as opposed to an unrealistic, safe and secure cotton candy land where it is impossible to suffer even a grazed knee, God unavoidably created a world full of danger and hurt. The world is not a puppet theatre, but uncompromisingly the real, unlimited deal. As such, the world is not evil, it is just everything possible, a world where sooner or later everything that can happen does happen.

It is tempting to take this line of reasoning further and seek to completely unlimit and unfetter reality by arguing that it is not created or derived. That it is what most truly exists because it is not the *product* of a higher being who is said to be that which most truly exists. In which case, what is superficially labelled 'evil', both natural and moral, happens because there is no God. This is the simplest solution to the problem of evil *philosophically*, because it dissolves rather than solves the problem, but it is, of course, a solution that remains absolutely morally unthinkable and intellectually out of bounds to saintly philosophers.

Leibniz takes a somewhat different approach. He holds that God exists and that the world only *appears* to contain evil from our limited perspective. If we could see the world as God sees it, under the aspect of eternity, if we could understand God's mysterious ways, then we would understand that absolutely everything that happens in the world, however terrible it may appear to us, happens for a good reason. Leibniz argues in his

Theodicy: Essays on the Goodness of God, the Freedom of Man and the Origin of Evil that this world, the actual world, must be the *best of all possible worlds*, because God, being both omnipotent and wholly good, would not have created a world that was less than the best.

Leibniz's thesis is famously satirized in Voltaire's philosophical novella, *Candide, or Optimism*. As Candide becomes increasingly disillusioned by the terrible pain, hardship and cruelty he witnesses and suffers, he is constantly reminded by his mentor, the absurd, idealistic, ever optimistic follower of the Leibnizian philosophy, Dr Pangloss, that 'All is for the best in the best of all possible worlds' (*Candide*, p. 21).

5

Conclusions

It was not difficult for us to say in broad terms what God, if he exists, must be like. In the words of Anselm, God must be 'Something than which nothing greater can be thought' (*Proslogion*, p. 7), otherwise he is not the supreme being. God, to be worthy of the name, must not only be the best that there is, but the best that is possible. The divine attributes of omnipotence, omniscience, omnipresence and even omnibenevolence were unfolded in reasonably short order from this initial premise, perhaps because in the end we were doing nothing more than extensively defining the meaning of a word.

Establishing what belongs to the word or idea *God*, and even where that idea comes from, was a relatively unproblematic task. Far more problematic was the whole thorny issue of the existence or non-existence of God, which, by raising real philosophical difficulties, obliged us to resort to some pretty tough philosophizing in response. It is hardly surprising that over half this book was taken up by that task.

When I told my good friend the philosopher N. J. H. Dent that I was writing a book about God, he responded dryly with, 'I hope he appreciates the attention.' As Dent understands, I do not know if God appreciates the attention, or indeed if he is offended by it, because I still do not know, despite having investigated the matter in some depth, whether or not God exists. Some readers will undoubtedly want to draw a different conclusion from these pages to satisfy their own theistic or atheistic leanings, but in my view, nothing that I have said in this book, no argument that I unearthed while researching it, no position that I have ever come across in my years as a philosopher, proves or disproves the existence of God. I can give only this verdict: God may or may not exist.

Some religious people are in the habit of mistaking the reservation that God may, after all, exist – a purely philosophical reservation based entirely on ever cautious scepticism – for some kind of *evidence* that he does exist. In doing this they are playing fast and lose with reason and logic because it is not evidence for the existence of x that nobody has ever disproved the existence of x. That nobody has disproved that there is life on Jupiter, for example, cannot by itself be taken to suggest that there is life on Jupiter. That nobody has disproved there is life on Jupiter simply means that life on Jupiter remains a *possibility*.

When a case is inconclusive it is inconclusive. Inconclusive means no conclusion can be drawn either way. Inconclusive does not mean everyone can go off and draw their own conclusions. People will, of course, go off and draw their own conclusions on any and every issue, that is human nature, but such so-called conclusions are really only speculations that people embrace for personal motives as though they were conclusions. They are really nothing but prejudices.

At the risk of repeating myself, I must say that having weighed all the main arguments for God's existence, and all the main objections to those arguments, my very agnostic conclusion is that it is not possible to know either that God exists or that he does not exist. With specific regard to arguments for God's existence, there certainly does not appear to be any incontrovertible proof, evidence or demonstration of God's existence to be found in the realms of logic, philosophy, theology or science. Not one of the theistic arguments – ontological, cosmological, teleological or moral – delivers absolute certainty. There is no argument for God's existence so strong that sound objections cannot be raised against it. There is no theistic theory concerning the origins and nature of the universe that succeeds in entirely ruling out alternative secular theories.

As for secular theories, they have the advantage of being backed by integrated scientific evidence. They are supported by what is observable and testable, whereas theistic theories always ultimately depend on metaphysical speculation that by definition exceeds the bounds of empirical knowledge, metaphysical speculation that makes progress only by craftily assuming beforehand what it is trying to prove.

Secular theories of the universe cannot prove God does not exist. God, if he exists, is transcendent, and therefore beyond the reach of scientific proof or disproof. Secular theories are, however, doing away with the *need* for God as an explanation of how things are in the world and how they came to be the way they are. God himself may or may not exist, but what is not in doubt is that the old *God of the gaps* has been looking increasingly illusory since the Enlightenment. As Nietzsche famously puts it, 'God is dead. God remains dead. And we have killed him. …What was holiest and mightiest of all that the world has yet owned has bled to death under our knives' (*The Gay Science*, 125, p. 181).

Throughout this book, in various ways, I have repeated the mantra of that great Enlightenment figure, David Hume, the mantra of empiricism and positivism generally, that nothing genuinely meaningful can be said that is not based either upon pure logical and mathematical reasoning or upon the evidence of the senses. This is the principle know as *Hume's fork*, his distinction between relations of ideas and matters of fact, these days referred to as the distinction between analytic and synthetic propositions. Metaphysics, which includes all the key propositions that comprise the theistic arguments, is neither purely logical or purely based on sensory evidence. It is therefore, according to the dictates of Hume's principle, essentially meaningless. Of the desire to say something metaphysical, Wittgenstein says:

> The correct method in philosophy would really be the following: to say nothing except what can be said, i.e. propositions of natural science – i.e. something that has nothing to do with philosophy – and then, whenever someone else wanted to say something metaphysical, to demonstrate to him that he had failed to give a meaning to certain signs in his propositions. Although it would not be satisfying to the other person – he would not have the feeling that we were teaching him philosophy – *this* method would be the only strictly correct one. (*Tractatus Logico-Philosophicus*, prop. 6.53)

Intriguing though metaphysics may be, when all is said and done, it is an exercise in idle speculation that is incapable of establishing the truth or falsehood of any declaration that it makes. The central problem of metaphysics, of all ruminating about the existence of a supreme metaphysical being, is the problem of *verification*. Metaphysical propositions, such as 'God exists' or 'God does not exist', being neither logical or empirical propositions, cannot be verified as true or false. Hence, the only thing that metaphysical reasoning can ever really achieve is to reveal that metaphysical reasoning goes nowhere or, at best, runs in circles of its own creation. In so far as much of the history of philosophy has been the history of metaphysics, particularly metaphysical theology, philosophy has largely been a trial and error exercise in discovering the strict limits of knowledge and reason by trying in vain to go beyond them.

Of the many thinkers who accept that it is not possible to know whether or not God exists, some argue that as God *may* exist it is of vital importance for people to live their lives as though he does exist. If a person is absolutely certain that there is no God then he must live as an atheist. But it is not absolutely certain that there is no God. There may be a God, in which case, so it is argued, it is better to live as a believer in God than as an agnostic.

Even if agnosticism is the only reasonable *philosophical* position, for a person to live his life as an agnostic, sitting on the fence refusing to embrace what he accepts is at least possible, is for him to value avoidance of philosophical error above what willing himself to faith in God might bring in terms of purpose, meaning, grace and salvation.

The best-known formulation of this line of reasoning is know as *Pascal's wager*, after the seventeenth-century French philosopher and mathematician, Blaise Pascal. In his *Pensées*

(*Thoughts*), Pascal argues that as we cannot know whether or not God exists, we are confronted with the need to make a decision about how we should live on the basis of a calculation of risks. Pascal argues that any wise person will gamble on living as though God exists because if God exists he will gain eternal salvation, whereas if God does not exist he will lose only a few worldly pleasures. Only a fool will gamble on living as though God does not exist because if he is wrong and God exists he will lose eternal salvation and gain only a few worldly pleasures. Pascal says:

> Do not condemn as wrong those who have made a choice, for you know nothing about it. 'No, but I will condemn them not for having made this particular choice, but any choice, for, although the one who calls heads and the other one are equally at fault, the fact is that they are both at fault: the right thing is not to wager at all.' Yes, but you must wager. There is no choice, you are already committed. Which will you choose then? … Since you must necessarily choose, your reason is no more affronted by choosing one rather than the other. That is one point cleared up. But your happiness? Let us weigh the gain and the loss involved in calling heads that God exists. Let us assess the two cases: if you win you win everything, if you lose you lose nothing. Do not hesitate then; wager that he does exist. (*Pensées,* pp. 122–3)

The nineteenth-century American pragmatist philosopher, William James, argues along similar lines in his brilliantly eloquent paper, 'The Will to Believe'. For James, however, it is not simply a matter of what a person stands to lose or gain after he dies, but a matter of how having faith or lacking faith affects him right now if God exists. If God exists and he has faith then he immediately gains 'a certain vital good' ('The Will to Believe', p. 204). A person, therefore, should will himself to believe without delay, rather than remain sceptical all his life on the grounds that a proof of God's existence is unattainable. The person who remains sceptical will lose out for sure, whereas the person who commits himself to believe may gain a great good. As James says:

> We cannot escape the issue by remaining sceptical and waiting for more light, because, although we do avoid error in that way *if religion be untrue*, we lose the good, *if it be true*, just as certainly as if we positively chose to disbelieve. It is as if a man should hesitate indefinitely to ask a certain woman to marry him because he was not perfectly sure that she would prove an angel after he brought her home. Would he not cut himself off from that particular angel possibility as decisively as if he went and married someone else? ('The Will to Believe', pp. 204–5)

James warns that to adhere to scepticism for the sake of avoiding error is, in many areas of life, not least the spiritual, to throw away chances to be a winner.

The major sticking point for an agnostic when it comes to willing himself to believe in God, when it comes to *choosing* to believe in God, is how he makes himself believe if he is just not certain. Belief is surely not a matter of choice, but a matter of what the evidence dictates. How does a person make himself believe it is raining outside if he does not know, being cooped up inside, whether or not it is raining outside? Surely, all he can believe is that he does not know.

Actually, there are times when belief is a matter of choice. A person can choose to believe in himself, to believe in his ability to complete a task and so on. To a great extent, for a person to believe he is confident is for him to be confident. Such is the nature of self-confidence. Or a person can choose to trust another, to show belief in another by his behaviour towards that other person, when there is no evidence that that other person is or is not trustworthy. At times, trusting another person is the only way to find out that they are trustworthy. The notion of trust, of choosing to trust and place faith in another, is at the heart of James' example of marriage. Marriage is always something of a leap of faith, as it is not possible for a person to obtain cast iron guarantees that marrying would be a good thing for him to do.

Pascal argues, as does the church, that if a person lives as though he has religious faith, he will eventually acquire religious faith. A life of religious habits and rituals will eventually still the nagging voice of doubt. And if doubts remain, well, at least he is pleasing God by trying if God exists. Pascal says:

> You want to find faith and you do not know the road. You want to be cured of unbelief and you ask for the remedy: learn from those who were once bound like you and who now wager all they have. These are people who know the road you wish to follow, who have been cured of the affliction of which you wish to be cured: follow the way by which they began. They behaved just as if they did believe, taking holy waters, having masses said, and so on. That will make you believe quite naturally, and will make you more docile. (*Pensées,* pp. 124–5)

In James' view, Pascal is rather cynically recommending behaviour that lacks sincerity, a calculating, cold-hearted response to a clinical assessment of risks. Ridiculing Pascal, James says:

> We feel that a faith in masses and holy water adopted wilfully after such a mechanical calculation would lack the inner soul of faith's reality; and if we were ourselves in the place of the Deity, we should probably take particular pleasure in cutting off believers of this pattern from their infinite reward. ('The Will to Believe', p. 189)

James appears to recommend instead the more subtle approach of determining oneself to see the world from a spiritual or religious point of view, to set aside scepticism in favour of wilfully interpreting phenomena such as love, morality and beauty as *sacred*: as having religious significance. We are never passive in the way we encounter the world, we always perceive it to some extent according to our own emotions and values, so it is quite possible for us to perceive the world and respond to the world from the point of view of *religious* emotions and values.

Why, it can be asked, is it important to have religious belief? Surely, what matters is that one is a good person, and one can be a good person without believing in God. If there is a moral God who judges us, then surely he judges us by how moral we are, not by how much we seek to believe in him, worship him, follow petty rules in his name and generally bother him. In which case, a moral atheist, a good, kind and generous atheist, of which there are many, may be building a more sturdy stairway to heaven than a cruel, bigoted, mean-minded, sanctimonious, religious zealot, of which there are also many.

If, like me, you think you can probably not help being an agnostic, it might nonetheless be prudent and wise, and would certainly do no harm, for you to be more ethical, if you are not already perfectly ethical already that is.

As for worshipping God, I may be wrong, but I cannot see that if God exists he requires or appreciates all that undignified grovelling, praising and pleading. As ever, my problem is not with God but with organized religion, which does not have much to do with God in reality, other than to give the old guy a bad name.

BIBLIOGRAPHY

Adams, Douglas, *The Hitchhiker's Guide to the Galaxy: A Trilogy in Four Parts* (London: Pan, 1992).

Alexander, Mrs Cecil Frances, 'All Things Bright and Beautiful', in *Hymns Ancient and Modern*, second edition, ed. William Henry Monk (London: William Clowes and Sons, 1875).

Anselm, *Proslogion with the Replies of Gaunilo and Anselm*, trans. Thomas Williams (Indianapolis, IN: Hackett, 2001).

Aquinas, Thomas, *Summa Theologiae, Questions on God*, ed. Brian Davies and Brian Leftow (Cambridge: Cambridge University Press, 2006).

Aristotle, *Physics*, trans. Robin Waterfield (Oxford: Oxford World's Classics, 2008).

Burns, Robert, 'Man was made to Mourn', in Burns, *Poems, Chiefly in the Scottish Dialect* (London: Penguin, 1999).

Cicero, Marcus Tullius, *The Nature of the Gods*, trans. P. G. Walsh (Oxford: Oxford World's Classics, 2008).

Cole, Peter, *Philosophy of Religion* (London: Hodder & Stoughton, 2005).

Cox, Gary, *How to Be a Philosopher, or How to Be Almost Certain that Almost Nothing is Certain* (London and New York: Continuum, 2010).

Darwin, Charles, *On the Origin of Species by Means of Natural Selection: Or The Preservation of Favoured Races in the Struggle for Life* (London: Penguin, 2009).

Davies, Brian, *An Introduction to the Philosophy of Religion* (Oxford: Oxford University Press, 2003).

Dawkins, Richard, *The Blind Watchmaker* (London: Penguin, 2006).

Descartes, René, *Discourse on Method and The Meditations*, trans. F. E. Sutcliffe (London: Penguin, 2007).

Durkheim, Émile, *The Elementary Forms of Religious Life*, trans. Carol Cosman (Oxford: Oxford World's Classics, 2008).

Eco, Umberto, *Foucault's Pendulum,* trans. William Weaver (London: Picador, 1990).

Freud, Sigmund, *The Future of an Illusion*, in The Penguin Freud Library,
    Volume 12: *Civilization, Society and Religion* (London: Penguin, 1991).
Gaunilo, *Reply on Behalf of the Fool*, in Anselm, *Proslogion with the
    Replies of Gaunilo and Anselm*, trans. Thomas Williams (Indianapolis,
    IN: Hackett, 2001).
Hick, John H., *Philosophy of Religion* (Englewood Cliffs, NJ: Prentice-Hall,
    1990).
Hume, David, *Dialogues Concerning Natural Religion* (London: Penguin,
    1990).
—*Enquiries Concerning Human Understanding and Concerning the
    Principles of Morals*, ed. L. A. Selby-Bigge (Oxford: Oxford University
    Press, 1975).
—*A Treatise of Human Nature*, ed. L. A. Selby-Bigge (Oxford: Oxford
    University Press, 1978).
Irenaeus, *Against Heresies*, ed. Alexander Roberts and James Donaldson
    (London and New York: Createspace, 2010).
James, William, 'The Will to Believe', in *Pragmatism: The Classic Writings*
    (Indianapolis, IN: Hackett, 1982).
Kant, Immanuel, *Critique of Practical Reason*, trans. Mary Gregor
    (Cambridge: Cambridge University Press, 1997).
—*Critique of Pure Reason*, trans. Norman Kemp Smith (London:
    Macmillan, 2003).
Leibniz, Gottfried Wilhelm, *Principles of Nature and of Grace, Founded
    on Reason*, in *Leibniz: Philosophical Writings*, ed. G. H. R. Parkinson
    (London: Everyman's Library, J. M. Dent, 1990).
—*Theodicy: Essays on the Goodness of God, the Freedom of Man and the
    Origin of Evil* (Charleston, SC: BiblioBazaar, 2007).
Mackie, J. L., *Ethics: Inventing Right and Wrong* (London: Penguin,
    1990).
—'Evil and Omnipotence', in *Mind*, Vol. 64, Issue 254, April 1955
    (Oxford: Oxford University Press, 1955).
—*The Miracle of Theism: Arguments for and against the Existence of God*
    (Oxford: Oxford University Press, 1982).
Marx, Karl, *Critique of Hegel's 'Philosophy of Right'*, ed. Joseph O'Malley
    (Cambridge: Cambridge University Press, 1982).
Mill, John Stuart, *On Liberty*, in *On Liberty and Other Essays* (Oxford:
    Oxford World's Classics, 1998).

—*Utilitarianism*, in *On Liberty and Other Essays* (Oxford: Oxford World's Classics, 1998).

Mounce, H. O., 'Morality and Religion', in *Philosophy of Religion: A Guide to the Subject*, ed. Brian Davies (London: Mowbray, 1998).

Nietzsche, Friedrich, *A Nietzsche Reader*, selections trans. R. J. Hollingdale (London: Penguin, 2004).

—*Beyond Good And Evil: Prelude To A Philosophy of the Future*, trans. R. J. Hollingdale (London: Penguin, 2003).

—*Daybreak: Thoughts on the Prejudices of Morality*, trans. R. J. Hollingdale (Cambridge: Cambridge University Press, 1997).

—*The Gay Science*, trans. Walter Kaufmann (New York: Vintage, 1974).

Paley, William, *Natural Theology, or Evidence of the Existence and Attributes of the Deity, Collected from the Appearances of Nature*, ed. Matthew D. Eddy and David Knight (Oxford: Oxford World's Classics, 2008).

Pascal, Blaise, *Pensées*, trans. A. J. Krailsheimer (London: Penguin, 1995).

Plato, *Timaeus and Critias*, trans. Desmond Lee (London, Penguin, 2008).

—*The Republic*, trans. Desmond Lee (London: Penguin, 2007).

—*Euthyphro*, trans. Hugh Tredennick, in *The Last Days of Socrates* (London: Penguin, 1983).

Sartre, Jean-Paul, *Being and Nothingness: An Essay on Phenomenological Ontology*, trans. Hazel E. Barnes (London and New York: Routledge, 2003).

Simmons, Robert E. and Scheepers, Lue, 'Winning By A Neck: Sexual Selection In the Evolution of Giraffe', in *The American Naturalist*, Vol. 148, No. 5, November 1996 (Chicago: University of Chicago Press, 1996).

Southern, Richard W., *Saint Anselm: A Portrait in a Landscape* (Cambridge: Cambridge University Press, 1992).

Voltaire, François-Marie Arouet de, *Voltaire in His Letters; being a Selection from His Correspondence*, trans. Stephen G. Tallentyre (Charleston, SC: BiblioBazaar, 2009).

—*Candide, or Optimism*, trans. Theo Cuffe (London: Penguin, 2006).

—'Epistle to the Author of the Book of the Three Impostors', in *The Complete Works of Voltaire: Correspondence and Related Documents October 1770 – June 1771*, Volume 121, ed. Theodore Besterman (Oxford: Voltaire Foundation, 1975).

Wittgenstein, Ludwig, *Tractatus Logico-Philosophicus*, trans. D. F. Pears and B. F. McGuinness (London and New York: Routledge, 2001).

INDEX